PEACE CHILD

BY DON RICHARDSON

G/L
REGAL
BOOKS

A Division of G/L Publications
Glendale, California, U.S.A.

© Copyright 1974 by G/L Publications
All rights reserved.
Printed in U.S.A.

Published by
Regal Books Division, G/L Publications
Glendale, California 91209, U.S.A.

Library of Congress Catalog Card No. 73-90621
ISBN 0-8307-0278-4

Photos on pages 314, 319 and 321 by Don Richardson
Other photos by Fred Roberts

Dedication

To the host of men, women and children
who have shared their earthly substance
that the Sawi might hear—
we gratefully dedicate these pages.

Contents

Acknowledgments

My special thanks to Dr. Myron Bromley,
noted linguist and translations consultant
for the United Bible Society;
to Rev. George Lazenby,
author, mission leader and Vice Principal
of the Melbourne Bible College;
for their helpful criticism
of this manuscript.
My gratitude also to my wife, Carol,
for the many hours she spent
typing this manuscript.

Author's Introduction

The Sawi people of the former Netherlands New Guinea are one of an estimated four hundred tribes in the western half of New Guinea now called West Irian or Irian Jaya. Each of these tribes is distinct and unique, a little cosmos to itself with its own world view, its own set of legends, its own sense of humor.

In 1962, Carol and I went to live among the Sawi. As we studied their language, wrestled with the complex aspects of its grammar and became aware of the Sawi culture, we gradually became aware also of the world view of these people.

When we probed into the legends of the Sawi and studied their customs, we found that we were living and working among a people who honor treachery as an ideal. In many of the legends that the Sawi people tell to their children around the campfires, the heroes are men who formed friendships with the express purpose of later betraying the befriended one to be killed and eaten. The Sawi expression for this practice is "to fatten with friendship for the slaughter."

In recognizing that the idealization of treachery was a part of the Sawi view of life, we understood why we felt a certain culture shock in living among them. And it also helped to explain the sense of otherness we felt among these people. Yet we had been sent there by God to win them, to overcome within a few short years this idealization of treachery which had been part of their way of life over centuries, possibly milleniums, of time.

The key God gave us to the heart of the Sawi people was the principle of redemptive analogy—the application to local custom of spiritual truth. The principle we discerned was that God had already provided for the evangelization of these people by means of redemptive analogies in their own culture. These analogies were our stepping-stones, the secret entryway by which the gospel came into the Sawi culture and started both a spiritual and a social revolution from within.

As Carol and I ministered to the Sawi by means of the "peace child" and other redemptive analogies, we watched in suspense to see if the Spirit of God would actually use this means of communication for the regeneration of these cannibalistic, head-hunting people. He did!

In an age when all of mankind is rapidly becoming

interdependent within a single global community, cross-cultural communication unavoidably becomes one of man's highest priorities. *Peace Child* chronicles the agony–and the triumph–of our attempt to probe one of the world's most violent cultures to its foundations and then to communicate meaningfully with members of that culture.

The result, we believe, is an adventure in human understanding which will infuse the reader with an even greater and more compassionate regard for the earth's endangered minority peoples.

Don Richardson

Sentani, Irian Jaya
1974

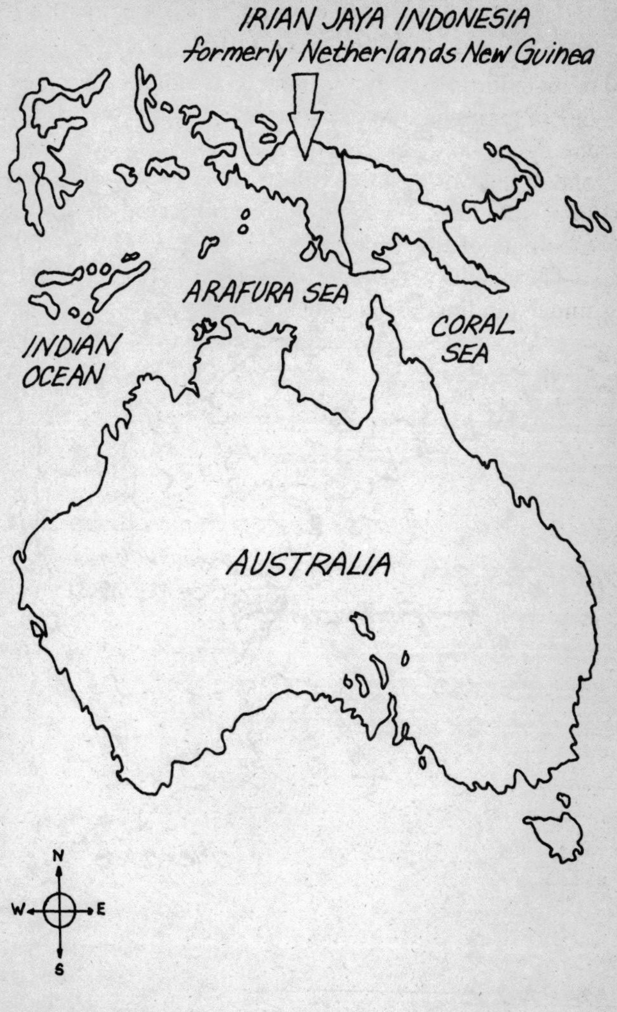

IRIAN JAYA INDONESIA
formerly Netherlands New Guinea

INDIAN OCEAN

ARAFURA SEA

CORAL SEA

AUSTRALIA

N
W — E
S

MAP NO. 1
Irian Jaya in relation to Australia

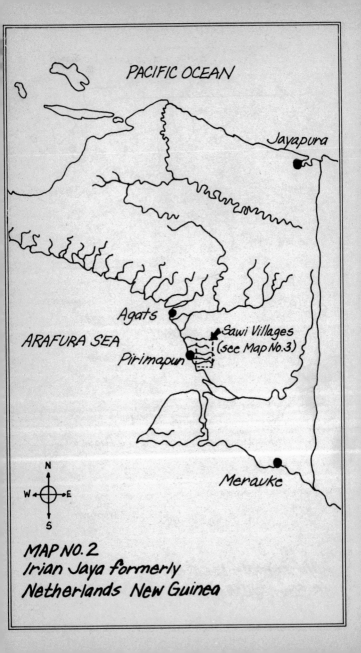

PACIFIC OCEAN

Jayapura

ARAFURA SEA

Agats

Sawi Villages
(see Map No.3)

Pirimapun

Merauke

N
W + E
S

MAP NO. 2
Irian Jaya formerly
Netherlands New Guinea

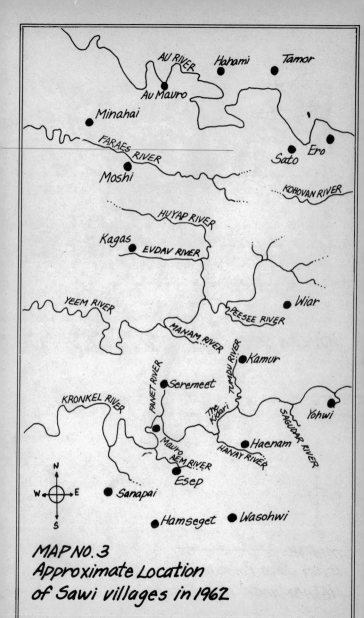

MAP NO. 3
Approximate Location
of Sawi villages in 1962

Part 1
World of the Sawi

1

Ambassador to Haenam

As the sun rose, Yae gazed down through the floor slats of his Mauro village treehouse at the dark surface of the Kronkel River forty feet below. His calm, black eyes studied the slow drift of leaves on the waveless surface. The leaves were drifting downstream, but at a decreasing rate, evidence that the rising tide of the Arafura Sea, twenty-five miles to the west, was beginning to stay the seaward crawl of the Kronkel.

Soon the tide would reverse the river's current completely. For a few hours it would force the black, algae-stained Kronkel back into the immense womb of the south New Guinea swamp which had spawned it. Yae had been waiting for this moment to begin his journey upstream, aided by the current.

Yae's wife, Kautap, sat cross-legged by the central

cooking place inside the treehouse. Her youngest child, still unnamed, lay asleep on her lap, cradled in the tresses of her heavy grass skirt. Leaning over the baby, Kautap sprinkled water from a bamboo cruse into the white sago flour scattered on the bark pallet before her. Slowly she kneaded the flour and water into a paste, while smoke from the smoldering fire bothered her eyes.

Her older offspring, two-year-old Miri, was playing contentedly beside her on a woven grass mat. His only toy was a human skull whose sad eyeholes gaped vacuously at the smoke-blackened ceiling as it rolled about. Already polished to a bright ocher sheen by years of fond handling, the skull was kept as a memento of Yae's long-dead father, and also as a fetish to ward off evil spirits. But to little Miri it was only a shiny toy.

Yae spoke to Kautap without turning to her. "*Uvur haramavi maken; du famud, es!* The tide is about to turn; cook my sago at once!"

Her deft black fingers quickly worked the damp sago paste into a long, slender shape, wrapped it in *yohom* leaves, and laid it among the hot coals. Yae meanwhile donned his ornaments in preparation for the journey. He covered his naked loins with the kind of narrow grass skirt which, in the Sawi tribe, could be worn only by men who had slain an enemy in battle. Yae had slain five. He had taken heads from three of his victims, and this was indicated by the three bracelets of gleaming wild boar tusks which hung around his left elbow.

His prowess in hunting was displayed next by his

sudafen, a six-foot-long necklace of animal teeth which he draped in two loops around his neck. Each wild pig, crocodile, dog or marsupial he had killed had contributed one tooth to the necklace. Bands of finely woven rattan also were fitted tightly above and below the muscles on each arm and just below his knees. Into the pierced septum of his nose he proudly inserted a six-inch length of hollow bone carved from the thighbone of a pig and sharpened to a point on each end.

If he had been journeying to attend an all-night dance, there were other ornaments he could have worn as well—a flame-colored bird-of-paradise plume, a headband of gold and brown marsupial fur, a splay of white cockatoo feathers, as well as white and red body paint made from powdered sea shells and red earth. But Yae's mission was purely diplomatic and not festive, so he was content simply to adorn himself with the white and gold of polished bone and braided rattan.

Kautap used a pair of tongs to remove the sago loaf from the coals, brushed off the charred leaves, and handed the steaming "swamp bread" to her husband. Yae ate half and placed half in his small sago bag made of woven fibers, along with a chunk of pork which Kautap had earlier smoked over the fire. Hanging the bag from his shoulder, he drew his six-foot-long bow made of black palmwood down from the overhead weapon rack. One end of the bow was tipped with a needle-sharp cassowary talon, so it could be used as a spear in close combat. Yae also selected a handful of sharply barbed, bamboo-shafted arrows. Grasping both bow and arrows in one hand, he took lastly his paddle which, along with his war shield, drum, stone axe, spear, canoe and bow, completed the main hierarchy of his earthly possessions.

The paddle was a striking example of Sawi artistry. Fashioned from a single nine-foot column of dark red ironwood, it featured a wide rectangular blade engraved with exotic designs, and at the upper end of its shaft, a boldly carved ancestral figure. Above the ancestral figure, the characteristic wooden barbs and cassowary talon warned that Yae's paddle, like his bow, could also double as a spear.

Yae stepped out onto the porch of the treehouse. Around him the six other treehouses of Mauro village seemed to float in the morning's golden haze, awkward, humpbacked, loaf-shaped. They were all about forty feet in length, and ranged from thirty to fifty feet in height above the ground, soaring over the tangled underbrush on long spindly treelegs. In addition there were four longhouses at elevations of less than twenty feet.

Not all Sawi families had the incentive to build treehouses, choosing to leave themselves more vulnerable to surprise attack than were the treehouse dwellers, who commanded an easy view of all their surroundings. In a tall treehouse, women and children could cower in relative safety while their husbands, fathers and brothers rained arrows down upon an encroaching enemy, or even descended to the ground to engage the enemy in *waru mim*, "spear play."

As Yae began his descent of the long, vine-fastened ladder, Kautap raised her voice in complaint. "Why do you go so often to visit Haenam? Doesn't your skin feel uneasy going there?"

Yae continued his descent. "If I had no friends there I wouldn't go," was his only reply. The ladder sloped back under the treehouse for shelter from tropical downpours and for shade. Yae descended the entire length without once touching a finger to the ladder for support, balancing perfectly on each precarious rung.

Near the foot of the ladder his younger brother, Sao, sat hunched on a log trembling with malarial chill, trying in vain to eke enough warmth from the morning sun which now glared into the village, causing steam to rise from dew-wet foliage. Yae spoke comfortingly to him, but Sao could hardly answer, his teeth were chattering so hard.

A few yards downstream Yae's cousin, Wasi, and Wasi's three wives were loading their sago cutting instruments into a canoe for a trip to the jungle. Yae called to Wasi. "I'm going to Haenam. I'll return just after dark. I'm going to invite my friends there to come to our *bisim* dance when the new moon appears."

Wasi wished him well in his mission as he stepped onto the stern tip of his sleek dugout and pushed out into the channel. His three wives stood well forward in the thirty-foot craft, two of them with babies secured to their backs in small carrying bags fashioned for the purpose. The three wives raised their paddles simultaneously and plied downstream toward the mouth of the small tributary which would lead them back into the sago swamp. A reserve of hot

coals trailed smoke from a little bed of clay near Wasi's feet. With these they would later kindle a fire to cook their afternoon meal from the fresh sago they would harvest in the swamps.

Yae laid his bow and arrows in his canoe and embarked. With a strong, deliberate stroke he aimed the needle-nosed craft upstream, just as the leaves on the surface came to a full stop in their seaward drift. By the time he vanished around a distant bend of the river, the leaves were moving upstream after him.

Kautap watched her husband vanish, a frown of concern on her smoke-darkened face. Then the baby on her lap began to stir and cry. She held the child to her breast and gave suck, wishing that Yae would forget his ambition to form an alliance between Mauro and Haenam.

A flourish of screaming cockatoos took flight as Yae's canoe suddenly appeared from under the screening foliage at the river's edge, still bearing upstream. A crocodile dozing on the tip of a sunken log awoke at their shrieking, gaped openmouthed at Yae, and then belly-flopped into the water, waving his massive tail up to a vertical position as he plunged into the depths.

Yae glided on to the next bend and rounded it, reflecting once more on the series of events which had established him as Mauro's only ambassador to the upstream Sawi village called Haenam. Seven months earlier Yae had unexpectedly encountered

a party of five men from Haenam, while he was hunting wild geese near the source of the Aym tributary. Yae had immediately crouched in his canoe and reached for his bow, but the tallest of the five strangers had quickly greeted him.

"*Konahari!* Don't take your bow! I know you—your name is Yae, and I am related to you!" said the tall stranger.

Yae raised his bow anyway, but did not fit an arrow to the string. Instead he asked, "What is your name?"

"My name is Kauwan. I am the youngest son of your mother's stepfather," was the reply.

"Why have you come to the Aym River? No doubt you and your friends are spying," Yae challenged.

"Not so," said Kauwan. "This morning I wounded a wild pig and we have followed its trail of blood this far. See, there is a fresh blood mark on the grass and here are the tracks where the pig floundered in the mud not long ago.

"Come let me embrace you! We are relatives!"

Yae had heard his mother speak of Kauwan, but still he hesitated. Kauwan then took a small piece of sharp bamboo from his satchel, cut off a lock of his stringy black hair, wrapped it in a leaf and offered it to Yae.

Reassured by this generally accepted token of sincerity, Yae paddled closer, took the gift from Kauwan and dropped it into his satchel. By this offering Kauwan had demonstrated that he desired more than just a passing acquaintance with Yae.

The two men embraced each other while Kauwan's

four companions voiced their approval. Then it was that Kauwan made his proposal.

"Yae, listen to me. For a long time the Kayagar people from the east have been raiding us and we have lost many to their spears. Thus we want peace with Mauro so that we can come freely in this direction to cut sago on our western borders.

"I have persuaded the men of Haenam that we need one man to act as a go-between who can travel freely between your village and mine. Surely you are just the man we need. I am now appointing you as that go-between. If you accept, come to our village three days from now. I will be waiting to assure your safety when you arrive."

Kauwan's four friends added that they also would protect Yae's life with their own if necessary.

Yae's heart began to beat faster. His own clansmen in Mauro had also begun to complain about the overpowering raids they were suffering from the Asmat people to the west. If peaceful relations with Haenam were established, the mature sago palms presently locked away in the no-man's-land between Haenam and Mauro could be harvested freely, relieving his people of the necessity to venture close to the Asmat borders for food.

In time Haenam and Mauro might even decide to join forces and inflict decisive blows against both the Asmat and the Kayagar, gaining respite for both villages from both directions. As the main engineers of that pact, Yae and Kauwan could both hope to rise to new heights of prestige within the Sawi cosmos. Men with marriageable daughters in other Sawi clans would surely be inclined to promise some of their daughters to Yae and to Kauwan, bringing each of them nearer to the Sawi ideal of possessing a harem of five healthy wives.

Yae had already gained two wives, but to his deep sorrow one had contracted yaws and wasted away with smelly, dripping sores and died, leaving him with only Kautap. Since the death of his second wife, Yae's longing to replace her and gain still other wives had become a constant obsession. Now, suddenly and unexpectedly, the satisfaction of that obsession seemed within his reach, *if* he could bring himself to trust the promise of Kauwan and his four friends.

Yae eyed Kauwan critically. Kauwan's eyes shone with evident sincerity. The fact of his relationship to Yae's mother was a reassuring factor. He had also voluntarily committed a lock of his hair to Yae's disposal. As for his story about Haenam being harried by the Kayagar and driven further west—Yae had already heard by the jungle grapevine that this was true.

On the negative side, Yae knew there were a number of people from the Kangae clan in Haenam who still bore unsettled grievances against Mauro. Could he be sure that Kauwan and his friends would be strong enough to protect him if the Kangae faction should opt for revenge when Yae appeared among them? The four pig-tusk bracelets adorning Kauwan's left elbow showed that Kauwan was a warrior to be reckoned with. But perhaps Kauwan was related to the Kangae faction more closely than he was to Yae's mother.

Slyly, Yae questioned Kauwan to ascertain his relation to the Kangae people. Kauwan immediately guessed the purpose of his questions and assured Yae that the chief men of Kangae clan had already said they would accept some token redress in goods as payment without demanding a human life. A few goods would be a small price to pay for all that Yae hoped to gain from this transaction.

Still, Yae delayed his decision for one further test. He invited Kauwan and his four friends to accompany him for a brief visit to Mauro, that they might discuss this matter further. If they were willing to trust him for protection in such a venture, this would be further evidence that their longing for peace with Mauro was truly deep-seated.

Kauwan replied with a broad smile: "We would be happy to go with you, but our wives and children are waiting by the Hanai River, expecting us to return with pig meat. We must find our prey, butcher it, and pack it home before dark."

This was a reasonable refusal, Yae thought. Now he must make his decision without any further test. If he refused, perhaps later someone else from Mauro would be offered the same honor Kauwan was now extending to him, and would accept it with consequent favorable results. How Yae would chafe inwardly if that happened!

Conversely, if he accepted, perhaps he would walk into a trap and lose his life! Yae's insides churned with the suspense of the moment, the same kind of existential suspense that formed a key ingredient of the Sawi legends that had fascinated him from childhood. Now *he* was the hero facing the dread-loaded choice!

Suddenly the decision came to him out of the vortex of his uncertainty. He took the little bamboo cutting edge from his sack, cut off a lock of his own hair and handed it to Kauwan, who accepted it with a smile.

Then Yae reached forward, gripped Kauwan's forearm firmly and said, *"Sarimakon, es!* I will surely come. It is settled!"

"Then if we find the pig we are seeking, be sure I will keep half of its liver and preserve it for you to eat with us on the third day," said Kauwan.

Yae replied, *"Timin konahari!* Thank you, friend!" and they separated.

Having given his word, Yae had virtually sealed whatever fate was in store for him. Unless he had strong evidence of treachery, he could not now change his mind without being branded a coward! He must go to Haenam on the third day.

And he must go alone. No one else would dare accompany him without invitation. So much the better; if he bore the risks alone, he would not need to share his subsequent honor with another from his village.

2

Fattened with Friendship

The midmorning sun had drawn beads of sweat from Yae's forehead by the time he reached the entrance of the Hanai tributary leading into Haenam's territory. He left the shimmering two-hundred-foot-wide channel of the Kronkel and soon felt his skin cooling in the deep shade of the Hanai River's narrow jungle-walled course. He stooped to drink while still standing in his canoe, scooping water with his hand. But he did not drink the water from his palm. Rather he tossed each scoop into the air and caught it in midair with his mouth.

Any other way of drinking water from the river was beneath his dignity. It could also be dangerous. Harmful spirits lived in the river, and if one did not drink in the prescribed way, they might invade one's body through the act of drinking.

Yae straightened up, and his eyes probed the bushes overhanging the river ahead of him. There

26

it was! The leering skull of a hapless Kayagar killed by Nair, one of the most feared warriors of Haenam.

The skull hung suspended from a branch, its eyeholes filled with bright red seeds embedded in black tree gum, giving it a most menacing appearance. Fluttering feathers hanging from each earhole gave an impression of hair. Nair had hung it there as a warning to enemies of Haenam.

Yae smiled as he recalled how the sight of that skull had made the hair crawl on the back of his neck when he had made his first tense approach to Haenam seven months earlier. Steeling his will, he had forced himself to keep plying his dugout past the skull and eventually had broken out onto the grassy plain where Haenam presently resided. The people had regarded his lone approach calmly, while Kauwan stood at the water's edge, welcoming him with outstretched arms.

As Yae beached his canoe and stepped ashore, Kauwan had suddenly lifted his bow and a handful of arrows out of a bush. Separating one arrow from the others and waving it in his right hand, he had turned his back toward Yae and faced his own people. With a mighty guttural shout he then leaped straight in the air and began to race back and forth between Yae and his own people.

He shrieked a formidable challenge, punctuating it with fierce grunts of simulated anger. "My friend is welcome! He has come because I myself invited him! Who is there who might want to harm him? He will not be harmed! My hand is strong!"

This was a customary display of force called *sara-*

von, a means of reassuring a guest and at the same time giving pause to anyone who might intend hostility. Without this display of *saravon*, Yae would have felt very uneasy indeed. The men of Haenam had watched calmly from their porches. Most of them were sitting with one leg flat on the floor and one knee upright, each one resting his chin on the upright knee.

After the *saravon*, Kauwan had embraced Yae warmly. The other men of Haenam then descended one by one from their houses and followed Kauwan's example in embracing him—except the men of Kangae, who were waiting for reparation before they expressed any good feelings toward the stranger.

Kauwan had led Yae up into the Haenam manhouse, the eighty-foot-long chamber which was the central structure of the village and where women might enter only by invitation. Kauwan had given Yae the place of honor on a new grass mat in the center of the long, rambling structure.

Soon Yae was surrounded by a circle of some twenty of Haenam's leading warriors, men like Maum, Giriman, Mahaen, Nair, Kani and Warahai, men whose names were feared by Sawi, Kayagar and Asmat alike. They had taken turns plying him with polite questions about his relatives. Behind them sat the younger men listening in respectful silence. Presently freshly toasted sago grubs cooked by the women in the family houses were brought in and served to Yae on a platter rich with intricate ancestral designs. He had waited courteously until his hosts had also been served and then began to eat with them.

Yae had noticed that gradually the conversation had turned to the matter of payment for the still unavenged grievances the Kangae clan held against Mauro. But Yae was ready. He had produced from his sack a number of stone axeheads, large sea shells, and other valuables which people of his village had sent with him to settle their debts with the Kangae clan.

A man named Giriman grinned with pleasure as he had gathered up the treasures and carried them out to the Kangae people, who were still waiting in their homes until payment was made. Meanwhile Kauwan produced the chunk of smoked pig's liver he had promised to reserve for Yae, and Yae had placed it in his sack to eat later.

Soon Giriman returned with the people of Kangae, who had touched hands with Yae and assured him that they had accepted the payment. They then joined the assembly, listening eagerly to every word.

Next followed a period when the Haenam people had heaped compliments upon Yae, saying they had heard of his prowess in fighting and hunting. After this the conversation turned to the wretchedness of both the Kayagar and the Asmat and the need for common respite by both Haenam and Mauro moving closer together and away from their enemies.

Yae had then risen to his feet and expressed his desire to return to Mauro. As he did so, he had trembled inwardly, knowing that if there was any treachery afoot, this was the moment it might be manifested. But instead they had willingly escorted him to his canoe and shouted the Sawi farewell,

"Aminahaiyo!" over and over as he paddled down the Hanai River toward the Kronkel.

Yae still remembered his elation during the homeward journey that day seven months before. He had arrived home at dusk, climbed up on the porch of his treehouse and shouted loudly to all his fellow-villagers in eloquent Sawi idiom:

"Where is the anger Haenam has felt toward us? Today I have broken off all the tongues of anger! Today I have sewn up the trail to Haenam which had fallen into disrepair. I have sprinkled cool water (peace) in the midst of our villages!"

He had then punctuated his speech with the Sawi cry of triumph—"EEEHAAA!" and listened with pleasure to the excited murmur of conversation his speech aroused in all the lofty treehouses around him and in the lower houses below.

That was only the beginning. In the past seven months he had visited Haenam a total of ten times and every time he had been received with the same warm welcome. His confidence had increased with each successive visit until now, as he found himself approaching Haenam for the eleventh time, not a single qualm of unease bothered him.

He now knew most of the men of Haenam by name and felt as sure of their good will as he did of the good will of his own clansmen in Mauro. He was confident that on this very day some of them would accept his invitation to accompany him later as guests to an all-night *bisim* dance at Mauro. After that, they would begin working out plans for a combined raid against either the Kayagar or the Asmat.

31

As before, Kauwan greeted Yae at the river's edge and led him into the manhouse. Others, whose acquaintance he had formed, came in one by one and sat in a circle around him. The conversation waxed pleasant as usual, sprinkled with anecdotes and side-splitting laughter. Food was placed before Yae and he began to eat with his hosts. Then he voiced the invitation he had come to lay before them.

Giriman was the first to respond, "You have now become an old friend of mine. Certainly I will come to the *bisim* at Mauro!" Mahaen also gave assurance, as did Kauwan.

Soon a total of twelve men had accepted the invitation. Yae was delighted. Then they handed Yae a length of string made of twisted tree fibers and asked him to tie one knot in the string for each day they must count off before coming to the feast.

Yae accepted the string gladly and began to tie the knots. While he was preoccupied at this task, Mahaen looked at Giriman and raised his eyebrows ever so slightly. Giriman saw the signal and passed it on to Maum. Maum passed it on to Kani, and Kani to Yamasi. By that time all of the Haenam men present had noticed the signal. Mahaen slowly moved his right hand under the edge of the grass mat on which he sat and drew forth a long, needle-sharp bone dagger, carved from the thighbone of a giant cassowary bird.

Giriman, Yamasi and Maum stood to their feet very casually and pretended to stretch themselves, while drawing long barbed ironwood spears from the overhead weapon rack. Grinning wickedly at each other, they held the spears poised over Yae while he hunched over the string, tying knots. Others in the assembly likewise armed themselves. Stone axes and spears, bows and arrows appeared as if by magic from under grass mats.

Each man who was armed stood quietly to his feet and moved closer to Yae. The only host who did not arm himself was Kauwan. He simply leaned back against the sago-frond wall, smiling at Yae and maintaining the thread of conversation while Yae tied the knots.

Yae noticed it was gradually getting darker around him, and quieter. His skin began to crawl with an icy chill, but he forced himself to look up optimistically. First he saw the weapons, and then something even more horrifying—the eyes of his hosts. Every eye was riveted upon Yae, bulging with voracious anticipation, straining to observe the expression on Yae's countenance. Then they saw what they had been waiting for seven months to see—the change of expression on Yae's face.

Gloatingly their eyes drank in the spectacle of serene confidence being devoured by abject terror, of cherished hope unexpectedly stabbed by black despair. For months to come they would indulge in avid descriptions of every detail they were now observing in this moment of truth. They would strive to outdo each other in depicting how Yae's eyes became dilated, how his lips trembled, how his entire body broke out with cold sweat. The manhouse would rock with laughter at each oratorical nuance the subject produced.

As Yae sat transfixed, choking with terror, Giriman stepped directly in front of him, spear poised for the strike. Yae saw Giriman's mouth open and heard the cruel, hissing voice say, *"Tuwi asonai makaerin! We have been fattening you with friendship for the slaughter!"*

It was an old Sawi expression, terse, deadly, which expressed in three words one of the deepest undercurrents of Sawi culture—the idealization of treachery. It told Yae that the men of Haenam had intended to kill him from the beginning, but being confident he would return again and again, they had decided on a long-delayed execution. To have killed Yae in the early stages would have been to settle for a commonplace murder which anyone unskilled in treachery could have accomplished. But to sustain the deception of friendship over a period of months and then consummate it as they were now doing called for that special sophistication in treachery which was the elixir of Sawi legends.

The men of Haenam were fulfilling an ancient ideal. Yae also was aware of the same legends that now motivated the men of Haenam. His mistake lay in thinking those legends had become divorced from real life, in assuming that the political and personal concerns of the present moment were more concrete than historical imperatives.

While the spears still poised over him, Yae's brain began to grapple with his situation. Why had he ever come to Haenam in the first place? It was because he had trusted in Kauwan. Kauwan? Where was he now? Perhaps there was still hope in Kauwan!

A choked cry escaped Yae's lips. "Kauwan! Where are you? Protect me, Kauwan!"

Kauwan looked down at him from between two of the armed warriors. He spoke slowly and calmly and sarcastically. "I kept telling them this was bad, that you are my friend and they should not do this to you. But Maum here has promised me his daughter in marriage if I would keep silent. Too bad, my friend, I guess I'm not going to help you."

Yae screamed at him in anguish. "Don't say that, Kauwan! Stand by your promise!"

He tried to rise to his feet, but Maum's spear struck him in the side. A mighty roar of released tension reverberated around him, while other spears moved in closer. Yae sank to one knee and called again to Kauwan for mercy, while he tried in vain to pull the barbed spear out of his side.

Kauwan turned away and said simply, "You should have given me a peace child. Then I would have protected you."

At these words, a vision formed in Yae's mind, a pain-distorted yet tender vision of Kautap sitting cross-legged by the fire, with the still unnamed baby lying asleep across her lap. The baby! Only that baby could have saved him! But now it was too late.

A stone axe struck him from behind, just below his shoulder blade. He toppled forward onto the sago-frond floor, gasping in pain. An arrow pierced the back of his thigh, and its sharp prick aroused him to sudden rage. He roared to his feet, streaming with blood, and lunged at his tormentors as another spear pierced through the calf of his leg. They simply

gave way before him, shrieking with amusement, but still they surrounded him.

Yae fell forward again and found himself looking down through a wide gap in the still incomplete flooring of the manhouse. Fifteen feet below he saw chickens cocking their heads to look up, disturbed by the uproar above them. He remembered that he had left his paddle stuck in the mud by the river. If he could drop from the manhouse and get to his paddle, he might be able to use the spear end of it to take at least one life in return for his own.

He slid downward, head first, through the gap, but the spear which had pierced the calf of his leg caught on the floor poles on either side, leaving him suspended upside down. Writhing helplessly in midair, he could only wait while the occupants of the manhouse quickly descended the stairpoles at either end of the building and came running toward him, fitting bamboo arrows to their bows. Women and children also came running, delighted at this unexpected opportunity, for the victim was now within their reach as well.

While children shot their child-sized arrows up into Yae, women raised their sago-digging sticks to club him on the head. Village dogs darted in and out among the stamping feet of the tormentors, licking up as best they could the blood sprinkling down, emitting ear-piercing yelps whenever they were stepped on.

When at last Yae was dead, someone dislodged the spear from which he hung and let his body fall, crumpling bamboo shafts under it as it struck the ground. Warriors danced wildly around the corpse, shouting various victory cries, each one boasting of the part he had played in the treachery and subsequent murder. Some bent over and began pulling arrows and spears from the torn flesh.

Then came the tall, muscular warrior named Maum with a newly sharpened stone axe slung over his shoulder. As the one who had purchased Kauwan's silence, he claimed the right to take Yae's head. The others made way for him as he stood over the corpse and raised the axe high. Wide-eyed children winced as the axe fell again and again, slashing through the tendons and vertebrae until the head was severed.

Meanwhile Maum's friend, Warahai, drew near with his son, Emaro, beside him. Maum lifted the severed head high and held it in the direction of the boy. Warahai then turned to Emaro and said, "Your name is Yae!"

The name Emaro had been only a provisional name, to be used until such time as the boy could be given the name of a victim killed especially for him. While his close associates would still occasionally call him Emaro, his "name of power" henceforth would be Yae. Whatever supernatural power had attended Yae would henceforth be added to the life force of the boy named after him.

Maum then sent word to a woman named Anai that Yae's jawbone would be given to her to hang around her neck during the celebrations called *eren* which customarily followed the taking of a head. When the woman received the message she cried out in jubilation and danced to celebrate her great honor.

When Yae's corpse had ceased bleeding, a number of men lifted it and carried it up the narrow stairpole into the manhouse, leaving the dogs to lick his blood from the ground and from the bushes where it had fallen. In the center of the manhouse, banana leaves were first strewn on the floor and then Yae's headless corpse was spread out on the banana leaves. Gathering swarms of flies immediately descended upon the gaping wounds.

Yae's ornaments were claimed by various men and removed from his body. Kauwan had already gone to the river's edge and claimed Yae's elegant paddle.

Then three men whom Maum had appointed to cut up the body came forward with razor-sharp bamboo knives. Onlookers excitedly shouted their claims to various parts of Yae's body, and Maum gave approval to each claim in turn. Then the butchering began.

While the men were preoccupied with the butchering, the women, who could not enter the manhouse unless invited, took down drums belonging to their respective husbands, fathers and brothers, and began to dance back and forth beside the manhouse. Sustaining a high-pitched rhythmic chant, they pounded in steady unison on lizard-skin drumheads glued on with human blood. Their heavy grass skirts flounced in time to the brooding thunder of the drums. Yellow bird-of-paradise plumes flashed in the sunlight. The day was at full heat, and sweat streamed from every body. Naked children embraced each other, jumped up and down, or threw sticks in the air to work off the intense excitement which possessed them.

Those who had already experienced the taste of human flesh began to chide those who had not, assuring them it tasted just like pork or cassowary. Why should they choose to be *kerkeriyap,* "squeamish"?

Some of those chided replied, *"Fadimakon govay!* Certainly I will eat it."

Others giggled and said, *"Rigav bohos fat fadon, hava ke fadyfem gani?* Why would anyone want to eat human flesh?"

Eventually all would overcome their feeling of *kerkeriyap* and partake, if not on this occasion, then on some other. But no Sawi could ever forget the dread of that first eating of human flesh. It marked one of the major thresholds each of them must cross in order to know the ultimate essence of Sawi existence. In the day each individual ate of that flesh, it seemed to him that his eyes were opened to know both good and evil.

After almost every part of Yae's body had been dissected and placed on wooden grills to sizzle over the various cooking places in the manhouse, all the unmarried men descended from the manhouse. Together with the women and children they retreated to the edge of the jungle beyond the village.

When Maum saw that they were at a safe distance, he laid Yae's head on its side, took a narrow stone and a wooden mallet and crouched over the head. Another man held the head firmly while Maum pounded the stone tool through the side of the skull. Flies swarming on Yae's long black eyelashes struggled to maintain their places as the blows fell.

The young men, the women and the children had first vacated the area because it was *apsar*, "forbidden" for them to hear the sound of the skull breaking open. When the operation was complete they came flocking back to the area of the manhouse, and the celebration resumed.

Meanwhile Maum began excavating the brains from inside the skull by way of the opening he had forced. His friends brought leaves and wooden platters of various kinds to collect their share of the brains, to be eaten with the flesh when it was cooked. Maum himself would not eat of the brains.

After this, Maum performed a ceremony called *yagon* in which he hoisted Yae's skull on the end of his bow and braced his bow in slanting position extending out from one wall of the manhouse. Then the cannibalistic feast began, followed by the complex rituals called *eren*, during which the women were invited to stand in one end of the manhouse, while Yae's jawbone was presented to the woman named Anai, who hung it around her neck as a prized ornament.

Kautap, when her suspicion of her husband's death was confirmed, shaved her head, came down wailing from the treehouse and threw herself in the mud of the river bank, writhing in uncontrolled anguish. She also took Yae's stone axe and threw it in the river that his spirit might use it in the world of the dead. Other relatives killed the jungle pig Yae had tamed and raised especially for the planned feast with

Haenam, in order that it also might accompany his spirit.

Then the entire village began to wail over the death of Yae. Treehouses swayed as mourners stamped back and forth from end to end. For three months no drums sounded in the village out of respect for Yae.

As for Kautap, she composed a dirge, which she kept moaning over and over as tears streamed down her ash-covered cheeks:

"O who will deal with the children of
   treachery?
O who will overcome those who use friendship
   to fatten their victims?
O what will it take to make them cease?"

Deeply moved by her incessant repetition of this plaintive theme, Yae's relatives sat down to plan revenge against Haenam. The possibility of any other answer to Kautap's question was quite beyond their comprehension. And as word of Kautap's dirge filtered eastward through the jungle, Maum eventually heard it. By that time the dry season had ended, the relentless monsoon storms were swashing noisy blasts of rain against the sago-frond walls of the Haenam manhouse. The entire grassy plain around the village was flooded.

Maum smiled as the words of the dirge were repeated to him. His only comment was barely audible above the roar of the wind, "Who indeed can overcome us?"

Then he yawned and stretched out for a midday

nap on his grass mat, pulling half of it over him as a shield from the damp, cool air gusting through the frond wall. Yae's jawless skull, already polished to a smooth sheen, rolled against Maum's shoulder as he drew the mat over him. He took it and placed it under his head as a pillow and was soon asleep.

3

Shadow of the Tuans

The men of Haenam eventually gained respite from their Kayagar problem by renewing an old alliance with two other Sawi-speaking villages, Yahamgit and Yohwi. Together these three inflicted heavy losses upon the Kayagar who live near the headwaters of the Kronkel, thus persuading the latter to sue for a period of peace. Mauro, similarly, successfully formed an alliance with Esep, Sanapai, Tiro and Wasohwi and managed to even their score against the Asmat-speaking villages near the mouth of the Kronkel.

To avenge the death of Yae, the men of Mauro made still further use of their alliance with Esep. They persuaded the men of Esep to use their good standing with Haenam to lure a group of men from Haenam to an all-night dance at Esep. Nine men accepted the honeyed invitation.

As the dance waxed on through the black and peaceful night, the warriors of Mauro came like phantoms up the Aym River in their canoes and then fanned out in the darkness, forming a circle around Esep. At the first greying of dawn they moved into close positions, and when it was light enough to distinguish between their friends in Esep and their enemies from Haenam, they charged.

Suddenly the chanting of the dancers and the throbbing of the drums faded to nothingness under the screaming crescendo of Mauro's attack. The men of Esep quickly climbed up into their houses and prevented anyone of Haenam from taking refuge in them. The nine intended victims tried to scatter through the shadows, as the sickening thud of spears striking flesh resounded through the village.

Five of the nine managed to escape, though all of them left livid trails of blood glistening behind them under the rising sun. Those who did not escape were Huyaham, Sao, Asien and Yamhwi. Esep and Mauro feasted royally on the flesh of the four victims, while Haenam spent several days and nights in rampant wailing for the dead.

After this the men of Haenam made foray after foray into Mauro and Esep territory, hoping to surprise some small group of men, women or children working at sago in the jungle. Unsuccessful, they later decided on a more indirect way of taking revenge. But in the meantime, three completely unforeseen developments occurred.

Once fairly peaceful relations with the Kayagar and Asmat were established, the various Sawi villages began to have frequent dialogue with their upriver and downriver neighbors. In the course of these dialogues, the Sawi noticed a new term they had never heard before. Both the Kayagar to the east and the Asmat to the west were beginning to jabber excitedly about something or someone called a *Tuan*. Since hardly more than half a dozen Sawi could make much sense of either of the two foreign languages, a long period of time passed before the Sawi were able to piece together a reasonable impression of what a Tuan was supposed to be like.

The consensus of reports seemed to indicate that Tuans were extremely large beings.

How frightening!

They were also known to be generally friendly.

This was reassuring!

Nevertheless, they were said to possess weapons capable of spurting fire with a sound like a thunderclap.

Seasoned warriors trembled!

They also were reported to be very much opposed to headhunting and cannibalism.

How fortunate that the headhunting Kayagar and the cannibal-headhunting Asmat were being exposed to that kind of influence!

Their skin was said to be as white as new sago flour. . . .

How unsightly they must look!

. . . and very cool to touch.

46

Could it be that they are not really human at all?

Their hair, furthermore, was straight or wavy, but never kinky, and they covered themselves with strange skins so completely that their actual persons were hardly visible!

How difficult it must be to know them as they really are!

Most informants affirmed that no female Tuan had ever been seen, though more distant sources claimed a few such existed.

How they must have to fight to obtain wives if there are so few women!

Almost as strange as the Tuans themselves were the objects they were said to dispense in trading. Chief among these were superior types of cutting instruments called *kapaks* for felling trees, *parangs* for slashing through bush, and *pisaus* for butchering meat. There were also tiny sticks called *korapi* which were excellent for starting a fire. Their *sukurus* could shave one's whiskers much better than bamboo knives! *Mata kail*, "fishhooks" and *kawas*, "fishline" made it possible to catch fish even in the main rivers, instead of having to wait until the water was low in the smaller rivers, when it was possible to spear fish or shoot them with bows and arrows.

Reportedly there were also *rusi*, in which one could see one's soul far more clearly than on the surface of a quiet pool of the swamps. Of special interest was a sheer white substance called *garam*, said to be far saltier than the charred residue of burnt sago fronds which the Sawi used to season their food. Still further, the Tuans were said to dispense *sabun* which, when mixed with water and applied to one's skin, could remove not only loose dirt but even skin-grease! Finally, the Tuans were believed to have various types of witchcraft called *obat* which could prevent fever and heal sores far more efficiently than Sawi witches could.

As more and more of this spellbinding talk about Tuans passed from village to village, the Sawi were not sure whether they would ever want to meet one or not. The material benefits were enticing, but what if unforeseen supernatural repercussions should develop? Long ago the forefathers of the Sawi had developed rapport with the spirits who lived in the rivers and in the jungle. "The spirits have accepted our skin-grease in their rivers," they would say. As long as this tenuous coexistence of spirits and people was maintained, the universe was in balance. True, terrible epidemics sometimes ravaged the villages, but the spirits kept them spaced out at wide enough intervals so that communities could survive.

But if a Tuan having no rapport with the spirits were to intrude strange skin-grease in the rivers and on the trails, the balance of the universe might be upset. The spirits might retaliate against the Sawi for this bold, unaccustomed intrusion into their domain, and the elders would have no methodology worked out for appeasing the spirits in such a unique situation. Possibly the Tuans themselves were spirits who would have to be appeased, and oh, it would take so long to try to discover the methodology for appeasing another set of spirits! It was demanding enough to survive in a dualistic spirits-and-people universe—how would the villages fare in a new tripartite spirits-Tuans-people universe?

This was the crucial question which began to occupy the minds of the Sawi, the more so as the Kayagar and the Asmat continued to expostulate on the strange wonders called Tuans. It was an entirely new kind of question, one their ancestors presumably never had to face. For this reason there was nothing in Sawi legends which could guide this present generation in its approach to the Tuan question. They were on their own, and they felt themselves trembling under the responsibility of a decision which could dramatically affect their own destinies and the fate of their little ones.

The crisis deepened very suddenly the day the second unforeseen development caught the Sawi by surprise. Haenam had moved to a new location on the tributary called Sagudar which was very close to the region of the Kayagar. One day a canoe loaded with husky, heavy-jawed Kayagar came down the river with an Atohwaem warrior named Hadi on board. Hadi was fluent in three languages: Atohwaem, Kayagar, and Sawi.

As the canoe approached Haenam, Hadi called out excitedly in Sawi. "These Kayagar men have something very special to show you!"

The warriors of Haenam came down slowly out of their houses as Hadi leaped ashore. Behind him a Kayagar named Hurip bent down and picked up a strange object lying at his feet in the canoe. His eyes gleamed with amusement as he observed the astonishment on the faces of the Sawi. He raised the object over his head. Then he opened his large mouth and spoke in the deep-chested, rumbling Kayagar language.

Hadi translated. "This is a *kapak!*"

The Sawi quickly crowded around, gaping. They stared at the object with the same degree of wonder an astronaut would feel upon discovering an artifact from an extraterrestrial civilization. The *kapak* was about as long as a man's hand with a shiny blade about four inches wide. The other end was rounded into a thick ring into which Hurip had fitted one end of a tapered ironwood handle.

Only vaguely did the wonderers see the object as having any resemblance to their own stone axes. That was until Hadi pointed to a young tree near the river's edge and urged Hurip to demonstrate what the strange object could do. Hurip stalked over to the tree, raised the axe far back over his right shoulder and struck a mighty blow deep into the base.

Hadi chuckled as the onlookers recoiled suddenly from the strange-sounding crack of steel piercing wood. Hurip wrenched the axe out, and with three more blows sent the tree toppling into the Kronkel. It was fully three minutes before the people of Haenam stopped shouting their amazement. Four blows with that object had felled a tree which would have required more than forty blows with a typical stone axe.

The Sawi invited Hadi, Hurip and the other Kayagar up into the manhouse. After all were seated, the wondrous *kapak* was passed around from hand to hand. Respectfully the Sawi caressed the fabled instrument, exclaiming over its hardness, sharpness and weight. They could hardly believe that a blade four times as thin as an average stone-axe blade could be used with such force and not snap or chip.

Hurip, puffed with pride at being the first to introduce an entire community to this totally alien wonder, then related how he had traded one of his children to another Kayagar far to the southeast in Araray village so as to obtain his *kapak*. The people of Araray had many such axes because they actually had a Tuan living among them, he said. Now all the Kayagar villages were traveling to Araray or to Kepi, he said, taking pigs or children to trade for axes and other Tuanian treasures. Some of the Sawi were about to ask Hurip if he was willing to trade his axe, but when they heard he had given a child for it, they desisted.

After a moment's breathless silence, a muscular young Sawi warrior named Kani spoke up from the back of the manhouse. "Hurip, why did that Tuan come to live in Araray?"

When the question was relayed to Hurip, he shrugged his hulking shoulders. "You must think the Tuans are the same as us!" he exclaimed. "If one of us moves to a certain place, you can know it is because he has much unharvested sago there, or because he is moving further away from his enemies, or because he wants to live where his father used to live.

"But the Tuans care little for sago. They seem to have no enemies. They are not tied to the land of their forefathers. They come where they want to come; they go where they want to go; they stay where they want to stay! No one ever knows what they will do or why. All we know is wherever they go, their canoes are heavy with axes like this one!"

The Sawi whistled to express their wonder, but Kani pursued his question. "If a Tuan were to come here, what would happen to us?"

When Hadi translated, Hurip answered immediately, "You Sawi are still cutting off human heads and eating human flesh. If a Tuan comes here, it's for sure you will have to stop that sort of thing. If you don't, he'll shoot fire at you! You will do *karia* instead! Then for your *karia* the Tuan will give you lots of *kapaks*, *parangs* and *pisaus.*"

None of the Sawi understood that *karia* meant "work." Some of them resumed their amazed whistling anyway. Others became suddenly quiet at the thought of never eating human flesh again, never cutting off heads and the possibility of being burned with fire.

Kani was one of those who did not whistle. He was reflecting upon the fact that he and his people had not yet taken revenge against Mauro for the slaying of his older brother Huyaham and the other three who had been speared with him in that nightmare trap at Esep. If Haenam was going to take revenge, it had better be swiftly, otherwise a Tuan might appear, in which case it might no longer be possible to take revenge.

Hurip, Hadi and their friends soon returned upstream, after promising the Sawi that if ever they had any spare axes to trade, they would let the men of Haenam know about it first.

Hurip and his friends had come for only one reason: to entertain themselves with the spectacle of an entire community stunned by its first vision of a steel axe. Unwittingly, they had accomplished far more!

Firstly, they had settled "the Tuan question" once and for all for the men of Haenam. Now at last these particular Sawi knew what they would do if a Tuan ever came their way. By sunset that evening they had arrived at a consensus of opinion which would soon find support in all eighteen villages of the Sawi tribe.

Secondly, they had persuaded the young man named Kani that it was time for Haenam to stage another enactment of the ancient theme called *tuwi asonai man.* More "pigs" must be "fattened for slaughter" to avenge the death of Huyaham before the Tuans appeared, just in case it should prove impossible to take vengeance after they appeared. And since frontal assaults against Mauro had failed, the fattening ingredient once again would have to be *friendship.*

But before Kani's murderous intentions found fulfillment, a third unexpected development was to rock the Sawi cosmos to its very foundations.

4

The Tuans Are Coming

As a seminomadic people, the Sawi never had to repair their houses. Whenever the long poles supporting their homes began to rot, they simply moved to a new location and built new homes.

When their residences on the Sagudar tributary began to decay, the men of Haenam entered into an agreement with another Sawi village named Kamur and established a new village together at the mouth of the Antap tributary on the northern side of the Kronkel, normally not Haenam territory. About four hundred people resided in the new community.

The various longhouses and two treehouses of the village were scattered along several hundred yards of shoreline, commanding a view of the longest straight stretch of the Kronkel to be found in Sawi territory. The people called it the *kidari*, which might be translated "the freeway." Elsewhere the Kronkel twisted and turned so tortuously that it was seldom possible to see more than half a mile of river in any one direction. Here on the *kidari*, one could stretch one's eyes along nearly a mile and a half of unobstructed channel.

It was here in this new location that Kani finally worked out the details of a master plan of ingenious treachery which he hoped would settle his obsessive grievance against Mauro. He knew the plan would fail, however, if he did not win the support of his peers in Haenam. Carefully he turned over and over in his mind the arguments he must use to win support. He weighed also the problem of who in his village could be trusted with knowledge of the plan. He sensed the danger that some would not favor the plan and would betray it to the enemy.

One morning as Kani sat puffing tobacco smoke through his long bamboo pipe, his daughter, Norom, announced, "*Navo, kabi sai!* Father, a canoe is coming!"

Kani turned and looked down the *kidari* as the approaching dugout veered toward the village. In it were eight of his closest fellow clansmen. Kani's heart began to pound with excitement for he had been waiting for these very men to return from their pig-hunting trip. Now at last they had come. Quickly he decided that on this very day he would confide his ingenious plan to them.

As his clansmen's canoe nudged in among the reeds at the Kronkel's edge, Kani lifted his pipe to his lips again. His eyes squinted slyly as he pulled the smoke into his lungs. No one in the smoky longhouse noticed that the corners of his lips were smiling around the mouthpiece of the pipe. Suddenly the smile froze.

At the river's edge, Kani's clan-brother, Sauni, lifted his spear-paddle to thrust it downward among the reeds into the mud. Then Sauni's arm froze.

Kani's other clan-brother, Mavu, having just stepped out of the canoe into the shallow water among the reeds, was bending down and gripping one side of the canoe, ready to heave the slim craft further in among the reeds. Mavu never completed the action. Instead his body suddenly tensed as he stooped, staring down into the reflections among the reeds.

Near the middle of the canoe, Maum, Yamasi, Haero and Sinar had also stepped into the shallow water and were starting to lift the heavy packs of freshly butchered wild pork they were bringing from the jungle. But the blood-red pork slipped from their hands and fell back into the canoe.

Naked brown children playing with bows and arrows fell quiet and stood staring with fear-filled eyes. The chattering of women died. The splitting of firewood ceased. The coughing of the sick sputtered to a halt. In the entire village only the crying of a single baby and the buzzing of myriad flies were left unhushed.

There was a sound! A distant sound. A strange sound. A pulsing sound! Kani frowned in alarm. It was as if somewhere a gigantic heart had begun to beat, causing the entire universe—the air, the water, the trees, the ground—to throb with its booming pulse.

At the shore, Maum's brain raced back over all his memories in vain. He had never heard anything like this before. If the sound were a steady, sustained

57

thunder, he might have said it was caused by thousands of gigantic breakers, stirred up by an unusually violent monsoon storm, pounding on the remote mud flats along the Arafura Sea. Or if its fluctuations had been irregular, he might have assumed that a distant thunderstorm was brewing.

But this steady pulsing boom defied any plausible explanation. Surely it could not arise from any natural phenomenon. It was too low-pitched to be the throb of man-made drums from a celebration in a distant Sawi village, and no animal known to the Sawi could sustain such a sound. Only one explanation was left to Maum—the sound had a supernatural origin.

Such a possibility could inspire only one feeling in the Sawi heart—terror! And Maum felt now the icy fetus of that terror swelling monstrously in the pit of his stomach, crowding the very breath out of his lungs, exerting a pressure that seemed about to cut off the beating of his heart.

Then the words Hadi had translated from the lips of Hurip came to him and he shrieked a warning to the village. *"Yot gwadivi saido!* It's coming to shoot fire!"

Kani dropped his pipe and leaped to his feet, tobacco smoke exploding from his lungs. He snatched up his bow and arrows with one hand and swung one of his children onto his back with the other. His wife passed another child to his older daughter, Norom, and swung still another child up onto her own back.

All around they could hear the tumult of scuffling, calling and crying which marked the beginning of a Sawi evacuation procedure. Longhouses swayed and

58

creaked as occupants rushed to the exits and clambered down stairpoles. Small children hung from their parents' necks as the latter carried grass mats and stone-age utensils bundled under their arms.

The people of Haenam and Kamur had been through this procedure many times before. The first sight of a flotilla of Kayagar or Asmat war canoes always produced the same frantic yet organized rush to the safety of the jungle. The difference was that on those occasions only the women and children fled, while the men remained to face the enemy.

Now, however, the men were joining the women in their flight to the jungle, because of the assumed supernatural nature of the approaching phenomenon. In addition to their children and their weapons, they carried also as many grass mats as they could manage. They were prepared to sleep in the wilds, if necessary.

While the women and children fled deeper into the jungle, Kani, Maum and the other men of Haenam and Kamur took up positions just inside the underbrush behind the village. Nervously they peered up at the scudding clouds above, at the quiet river, at the depths of the forest behind them, ready to flee deeper into the jungle at a moment's warning. Not far away a daring young Kamur boy named Isai disobeyed his older brother's command to flee and climbed a tree to look out over the underbrush at the river.

Once the screaming of women and children had faded into the distance behind them, the hidden warriors were able to hear again the pulsing sound. It was much louder now. The soft earth of the very swamp itself seemed to tremble in time to it. At first it seemed to originate on all sides, reverberating through the entire forest, but gradually they noticed that the sound was coming from the west. Yet its point of origin was also moving southward, and this suggested a dreadful thought to Kani. The source of the sound must be following a southward bend of the Kronkel River. If that were the case, rounding the next bend would lead it back northward again within sight of the watchers!

Presently the moving source reached the point where, Kani realized, it ought to turn northward again and grow rapidly louder as it approached their position. Tense fingers fitted arrows to rattan bowstrings, though none of the Sawi were sure they would ever dare to release an arrow at the approaching doom. Then, all at once the sound grew so loud that some of the warriors panicked and fled. Those who remained felt their skin turning cold, while the hair on the back of their necks seemed to stand out straight.

Then, before their unbelieving eyes, waves larger than any that had ever been seen on the jungle-sheltered bends of the Kronkel swept out from behind the screening foliage at the south bend of the river. *Ahos* trees, struck by the waves, began to sway and toss violently. In another second, the monster force creating those waves would sweep into view! Kani's heart almost stopped.

The two canopied riverboats churned around another bend of the Kronkel, their twin diesel engines throbbing almost in unison. Each advanced under a fluttering red, white and blue flag of the Netherlands. They had begun their voyage several days earlier at Agats, the nearest Dutch government post, located on the coast of the Arafura Sea about fifty miles north of the mouth of the Kronkel River. Their mission: to explore the little-known southern extremity of the Agats administrative district, which until now had been left without any kind of government supervision. They were also seeking a site for a new Dutch administrative post in the area, a center from which the Dutch police hoped to put an end to the ceaseless headhunting and cannibalism known to be rife in this wild area.

The probe had already spent several days following the serpentine switchbends of swamp-embedded rivers like the Kronkel, trying to locate centers of native population beyond the already known Asmat area. So far they had been quite unsuccessful. The savage inhabitants of this ungoverned inland area were generally far too wary to risk building their villages within sight of main rivers. Hopelessly fragmented into small units by their internal conflicts, most villages could not count on numbers for protection against outsiders, resorting instead to the camouflage of deep jungle hideouts. The Dutch military commander in charge of this exploratory mission could not know that already that morning he had passed near the secluded hideaways of four downriver Sawi villages, imparting terror to every soul who had heard the sound of his twin diesels.

As the two ships swung north again, the impressive treehouses of a new village suddenly loomed into view. Here is an exception, the commander thought, as he peered at the odd-shaped treehouses of one village which had dared to locate on a main river. Smoke still drifted up through the arching thatched roofs, but there was no sign of any inhabitants. They've fled into the jungle, he thought. The commander gave the order for the probe to continue upstream past the village. Perhaps by the time they had followed the Kronkel as far as it would allow and returned on the morrow, the people of this village would have recovered their composure enough to show themselves.

Meanwhile, the watchers in the underbrush were certain that the village they had just evacuated was about to be destroyed and that there was nothing they could do to protect it. What good would bamboo arrows do against two swift-moving monsters so immense that they made the mighty Kronkel seem barely wide enough to contain them?

As the two monsters drew nearer, Kani squinted in unbelief, for he could see several dozen men, their bodies sheathed in strange coverings, looking out from under canopies. Some of the men were black-skinned like himself, but a few had faces that shone like fresh, pink sago loaves glistening in the sun.

Kani drew the inevitable conclusion and exclaimed, "Tuans! The Tuans are coming!"

Wallowing in their own waves, the ships swept on past the twin villages and threaded their way down the long expanse of the *kidari*. Little Isai, perched among the branches of his lookout tree, felt his breath returning. Straining his ears, he detected the sound of low-pitched human voices mingled with the roar of the engines.

Then a man sitting on top of one of the canopies stood up beside the flag and waved toward the bushes, on the likely chance that human eyes would be watching. Isai felt that the man must be able to see him in spite of his camouflage of leaves and branches, and he cringed trembling behind the main trunk of the tree. How could their eyes be so keen?

That night the two ships stood at anchor under the stars, moored along the banks of the Kronkel, deep in the Kayagar grasslands. There hundreds of the people of that area—more accustomed to the comings and goings of the Tuans—gathered around the riverboats to trade fish, sago and pork for matches, razor blades, beads and tobacco. Yet even the Kayagar found the glaring kerosene pressure lamps unnerving and the blaring transistor radios incomprehensible.

And at the same time, further downstream the elders of both Haenam and Kamur conferred well into the night. Surmising that the two "super canoes" must be overnighting among the Kayagar and would be coming back through the Sawi area on the morrow, they were debating whether they should try to make some sort of contact with the awesome strangers, or just let them pass by as they had come.

Finally three elders of Kamur named Kigo, Hato and Numu volunteered to try to make a friendly contact. "Years ago we lived among the Auyu people far to the east," they said, "and we still remember much of the Auyu language. Perhaps some of these strangers speak Auyu. When they return downstream, we will stand by the mouth of the Tumdu tributary and wave to them. If they pull over, we will try to talk with them in the Auyu tongue."

The next day, while hundreds of Sawi eyes watched from the assumed safety of the jungle, Kigo, Hato and Numu stood fearfully by the mouth of the Tumdu tributary, trying desperately to control the knocking of their knees as the roar of the twin diesels came pulsing out of the east. It seemed like an age before the two monsters finally roared into view and came bearing down on the three men. Struggling to hide their timidity, the naked trio stood trembling with gifts of food in their hands, wondering if they themselves might end up becoming food for the approaching giants.

The three almost collapsed in relief when the first of the ships swirled past them, hurling its mighty wake at their feet. But then, as they stood waving tremulously, the second craft suddenly cut its engines and swung toward them! Nervously, Kigo started jabbering in Auyu, while Numu and Hato kept nodding their heads in support. Government officers peered at them curiously from under the canopy.

Then from inside the ship a friendly voice greeted them in Auyu, and the three felt every muscle in their bodies relaxing. Perhaps now there was hope they would survive this dreadful encounter! Friendly hands reached over the side of the boat, accepted the gifts of food and returned payment. In addition to the blackfaced Auyu speaker, Kigo, Hato, and Numu were aware of incredibly large, white-faced men uttering equally incredibly strange sounds with even more incredibly deep, bass voices.

These must be the Tuans! Their white faces seemed so terrible to look upon that the three savages could not bear to give them more than an occasional glance. But in another moment the boat reversed its engines, pulled away from the shore and was soon chugging noisily down the *kidari* after its brother.

Kigo, Hato and Numu, feeling somewhat faint from nervous strain, turned toward the jungle and saw the men of Kamur and Haenam emerging furtively from the bushes. Then when it was apparent that the two ships were already a safe distance away, the Sawi all ran excitedly toward the three heroes.

Proudly, Kigo, Hato and Numu held up the razor blades, the matches, the fishline and the fishhooks for all the wondering eyes to see. They still had no idea, of course, what these things were or how they could be used.

It would be several days yet before a well-informed Kayagar would come down the river and, in a most ostentatious manner, show them how to remove the red paper wrapper in order to discover the gleaming new razor blade inside! He would also show them how to slide the matchbox open, take out a match and strike it against the side of the box in order to produce fire! Then he would explain very condescendingly that it was necessary to put some bait on the barbed hooks in order to catch a fish! Then he would return upstream to laugh for days at the simplicity of the Sawi in not knowing such obvious details, forgetting that it had been only a few months since he himself had learned the same lessons.

To Kigo, Hato and Numu, however, the main value of these treasures was not so much their practical uses, but the fact that these were tangible trophies of their encounter with beings whom they regarded as belonging to a completely different race. The little curios were more than that. They were also concrete evidence that three brave Sawi had touched hands across a culture gap equal to several thousand years of human development.

5

The Legendmaker

So dramatic was the encounter with the two river boats that few of the Sawi could talk about anything else for weeks. Not long after, the villages heard a rumor that the same patrol had established a post among the Asmat at Pirimapun and this occasioned still further talk! Even Kani was completely distracted from pursuing his plans for treachery against those he regarded as his enemies. But not for long. The memory of the two ships soon began to fade. The old longings regained priority.

One day Kani's two wives went off along the mud banks of the river to search for shrimp at low tide. Finding himself alone, Kani invited Maum, Mavu and Sauni up into his home. He stuffed his pipe full of tobacco, lit it, and passed it around to them. As the sweet, humid smell of the tobacco smoke spread through the longhouse, Kani began to disclose his thoughts.

"So! The Tuans are coming among us already, and still we have not avenged the death of our brother, Huyaham. How do you feel about that?"

The others grew quiet, feeling slightly ashamed for having let all thought of that solemn obligation slip from their minds for so long.

Kani continued, "Perhaps you have long ago forgotten Huyaham. But as for me, I cannot forget. I say we must avenge him, even if we have to do it in the shadow of the Tuans!"

Kani breathed on his pipe while the three men searched his face.

"You want us to make another foray into Mauro territory?" asked Maum.

"We've tried that often enough," said Kani. "I have a better plan."

Sauni was first to reply. "Tell us your plan, older brother!"

Kani waved his pipe toward the south, in the direction of a distant Sawi village called Wasohwi. "The men of Wasohwi," he said softly, "are brothers to those who killed Huyaham. They also have a few friends among the Kangae people in the other end of our own village. Does that suggest anything to you?"

All three listeners smiled slyly at the obvious connection, but then Mavu frowned. "How can we get them to come?" he asked.

Kani replied, "We will announce an all-night dance and send them an invitation."

"But who will take the invitation to them? The Kangae men are friends with Wasohwi, to be sure, but they are not accustomed to going there on visits. Besides, they would surely refuse to cooperate in this."

"Our brothers of the Kangae clan must know nothing of this!" said Kani firmly. "We must allow them to think this is a sincere invitation. Not until they see the corpses of their Wasohwi friends lying on the ground will they know what we have in mind."

"Then who will go and bring the victims to us?" queried Mavu.

"Have you forgotten," Kani said slowly, "that one of our own clan is related to Wasohwi through his mother, and goes there freely to visit?"

All three listeners whistled in astonishment. "You must mean Mahaen!" Maum exclaimed. "How can you possibly persuade him to betray his own mother's people?"

Kani was ready with the answer he had prepared long before. "There is no possible way we can persuade Mahaen to do this thing," he said matter-of-factly, and then added in a mysterious whisper, "but there is a way we can compel him to do it." After another pause he continued, "Someone will have to impose the *waness* bind on him. Then he will do what we say."

The eyes of his three listeners grew round with awe at Kani's words. Had anyone ever proposed such a thing before, that the ancient custom of *waness* be invoked to compel a close relative to betray his own mother's people?

It seemed to Maum, Sauni and Mavu that Kani

was carrying the Sawi idealization of treachery to a new refinement beyond anything the ancestors had ever dreamed of, even in their most subtle moments. This meant that Kani was a potential legendmaker in his own right, and he was offering them the privilege of sharing with him in the making of this new legend!

The three men found themselves mesmerized by the uniqueness of Kani's proposal. Of course, the very fact of its uniqueness greatly enhanced the chance it would succeed. It had been a long time since Mauro had struck that traumatic blow against Haenam by killing and devouring Huyaham and his three friends. The men of Wasohwi by now had probably almost forgotten the event. Even if they did think of it, they would hardly suspect that Huyaham's relatives might sublimate their desire for revenge against Mauro into a covert plot against Wasohwi! They would feel certain that their friends in the Kangae section of Haenam would warn them of any danger there. And in the other end of Haenam, the division called Kubhai, they would be counting on Mahaen as their protector. Thus it was virtually certain they would accept an invitation if it were delivered to them personally by Mahaen. There was nothing in the legends to warn that a man might betray his own mother's relatives!

The crucial ingredient in the plan was, of course, the use of the old *waness* custom to compel Mahaen's compliance. The three co-conspirators were eager to hear Kani's ideas as to how this might best be accomplished.

70

Maum was first to express his curiosity on this matter. "Older brother, tell us; which of us do you intend should impose the *waness* bind on Mahaen?"

Kani smiled, proud of the ease with which he had drawn them into his web of intrigue. Now he was truly master of their attention, and he chose his words carefully as he proceeded to exploit their complicity. "It will not be one of us, my brothers," he said slowly, his black eyes darting from face to awestruck face.

He paused to let their curiosity reach a still deeper intensity, and then continued. "No, it will not be one of us. It will have to be your mother, old Wario!"

Mavu sat thunderstruck. Maum touched his finger-tips to his chest and whistled a long, low, descending note, a characteristic Sawi expression of extreme amazement. Sauni leaned his head back and moaned, "Wooooooooo," expressing sympathy for Mahaen, because of the shock that was in store for him.

All three men now looked at each other in mute acknowledgement of Kani's genius. Old Wario was none other than the mother of Waib, the beautiful young girl who had been promised to Mahaen, and who would later become Mahaen's fourth wife. If old Wario, as Mahaen's future mother-in-law, were to impose the *waness* bind upon Mahaen, the unfortunate fellow would be bound with an obligation more solemn than any other obligation imaginable within the Sawi universe.

Nothing could be more sacred to the mind of a male Sawi than his relationship to those who gave him their daughter or daughters in marriage. So great was a Sawi man's respect for his parents-in-law that he would not allow himself even to utter their names out loud. He would refer to them only by their title of *tade*. He would lavish gifts of fresh wild pork, or beetle grubs upon his parents-in-law with faithful regularity, often at the expense of his own family. In fact, his debt to his parents-in-law ranked higher in his mind than his debt to his own parents, or to his wife, or to his children.

In an almost totally barbaric society, there was always the danger that mutual hostilities would cut off the free exchange of marriageable daughters between opposite clans, thus threatening the existence not only of individuals but of the very society itself. Hence the collective instinct for self-preservation required that the highest priority be given to the parent-in-law/son-in-law relationship. Whatever other ties might be shipwrecked in the tides of savagery, the *tade-asen* relationship, as it was known in the Sawi language, must be preserved intact. For only as the social rewards of giving a daughter were secure would parents continue to give their daughters in marriage.

And Kani was now proposing that this noble ideal, which was intended for the preservation of Sawi society, should, through the medium of the *waness* bind, be subverted to the task of compelling a man to betray his own mother's relatives to death! Like a chess master inventing a new combination of moves in an old, old game, Kani was deliberately toying with diverse elements of his own culture and recombining them into a startling new variation of the ancient theme of *tuwi asonai man*.

Mavu, Maum and Sauni could not disguise their awe. They sensed they were sitting in the presence of a new culture hero, that if Kani's plan worked, a new saga would be born, a saga which, over a long period of time, would eventually be assimilated into the main corpus of Sawi legends. They knew also that as co-conspirators, their own names would surely be connected with that legend!

Kani himself felt a deep personal gratification in the prospects of his plan. His father Sauwai before him had been a legendmaker, a man whose exploits in treachery were often recounted around the night fires in many villages. Now the son was fulfilling, if not surpassing, the ideal established by the father.

Maum and Sauni, who also were two of old Wario's many children, and as such, future brothers-in-law to Mahaen, immediately gave their permission for Kani to approach their mother with his bizarre proposal.

Among the savage tribes of southwest New Guinea, women were no mere bystanders to the arts of cruelty. Whenever Auyu warriors, for example, returned from a headhunting raid, their womenfolk would welcome them by beating with sticks anyone who failed to bring back a human head! Among all the tribes, it was often the women who kept goading the men until they had avenged the death of loved ones slain in earlier outrages. Always it was the women who supplied that gratifying adulation which made the risking of one's life seem worthwhile.

Sawi warriors were especially fond of dragging wounded victims back to their villages in order that the women might have the pleasure of clubbing them to death with their sago-beating sticks. (It was forbidden, of course, for women to use or even touch a bow or a spear. If women ever became proficient in using weapons of *that* caliber, their own menfolk would be in danger! The various Amazon legends which abound everywhere in New Guinea were sufficient warning on that score!)

Finally, the Sawi *eren* ceremony, in which a girl or a woman was allowed to wear the jawbone of a freshly killed victim around her neck and dance in the manhouse, was the ultimate evidence of female emotional involvement in the practice of headhunting.

Whenever, on rare occasions, a woman played a significant or unique part in an enactment of the *tuwi asonai man* ideal, this was sure to be remembered in each narration of the story concerned. Old Wario was as knowledgeable as any Sawi woman in such matters, and Kani was certain she would not deny herself the place in the sun he was about to offer her.

———————————————

Old Wario, her head shaven in the manner of Sawi widows, sat nervously on the grass mat, weighing the suggestion which the four men, two of them her own sons, had just whispered to her. They waited.

She raised a pair of tongs and turned over the sago loaves she was baking among the hot coals of

74

a firebed. She looked out through the gaps in the sago-frond wall at the slender, beautiful form of her daughter Waib, who was standing in a dugout on the dark surface of the Kronkel, gleefully using the blade of her paddle to splash water on a playmate standing in another canoe.

Wario laid down the wooden tongs and looked straight into Kani's expectant face. "I have always felt very sorry over Huyaham, to be sure!" she said, and then added the fateful words:

"Call Mahaen!"

Mahaen climbed up into Maum's longhouse and took his place on the grass mat spread for him. He was a slender, wiry man whose tense, knotted muscles, pig-tusk bracelets and gleaming *sudafen* necklace warned of his considerable prowess in fighting and hunting. Maum, Sauni, Mavu and Kani sat down in front of him to draw his attention, while old Wario crouched behind him, pretending to mind the fire. Near her feet lay one of the sago loaves she had just finished baking.

Taking the loaf, she came up behind Mahaen and stooped beside the naked man on the pretense of offering the loaf to him. Distracted, Mahaen raised his hand to accept the sago. He did not notice the sudden gleam in the eyes of the four men who sat watching him and old Wario. Nor did he have time to notice that their conversation had stopped abruptly in midsentence.

There was a sudden quick blur of movement as

Wario, avoiding his outstretched hand, reached down and touched the sago loaf lightly against Mahaen's genital area. Quickly she leaped back out of Mahaen's reach, knelt facing him, and raised the loaf to her lips. Stark horror flooded into Mahaen's large black eyes as he saw Wario bite into the end of the sago which had touched him. Like an animal who suddenly sees it is trapped, Mahaen cringed.

Waness!

By this one dread act, Wario had abruptly shifted Mahaen's destiny in some new direction as yet unknown to him. There was no escape for him. By subjecting herself to the utter humiliation of eating sago which had touched Mahaen's private parts, Wario had imposed a formidable debt upon him, a debt infinitely compounded by the fact that she was his mother-in-law.

There was only one way Mahaen could cancel the debt he now owed to Wario. First he must ask her what he must do to atone for her humiliation, and then he must do it, no matter what it cost him. If he did not, Wario would continue to bear her shame and the entire community would be eternally offended at him. That the command she had in mind would be obnoxious to him was already clear, otherwise she would not have used the extreme measure of *waness*. It was the revulsion he would feel in obeying that still unknown command that would balance Wario's humiliation.

The five conspirators waited in silence as Mahaen stared blankly at the grass mat on which he sat. Hot waves of shame swept over him at the thought of his mother-in-law's humiliation. Finally, after several minutes, a curious, lost expression contorted his features as he looked at Wario's feet and uttered in a broken voice the words they were waiting to hear:

"What do you want me to do?"

The news spread like fire. First it burned the ears of the villages along the Kronkel River and then razed a path south to the banks of the Cook and over to the Juliana. Northward, it seared its way to the Sawi and Asmat along the Yeem. Finally, after it had spread its pall across the Faraes, it dwindled to a faint rumor and died on the banks of the Au.

It was shouted in Sawi, babbled in Atohwaem, thundered in Kayagar, twittered in Auyu, and mumbled in Asmat. It was the news of Mahaen's treachery against his own mother's people. For Haenam it was a new crown of infamy; for Wasohwi, a hell burning with sorrow and fiery indignation. Fathers, mothers, brothers, sisters, sons and daughters rolled in ashes, their voices hoarse with wailing, their eyes reddened with scalding tears.

Eight men from Wasohwi had trustingly accepted Mahaen's invitation to the all-night dance at Haenam. They arrived by dugout at sunset, just as the young men of Haenam, resplendent in paint and plumes, were beginning to rumble their drums for the dance. A large group of the most prestigious men of Haenam, led by Kani, welcomed the visitors at the shore.

Kani himself singled out a man named Fusuman and invited him to eat sago and beetle grubs. Fusuman obediently followed Kani up into the tall tree-house. Sauni, Warahai, Mavu, Maum, Boro, Yamasi and Paha likewise singled out their choice of the guests and led them to separate houses. There was not a hint of the treachery to follow. Even some of the occupants of Haenam itself were totally unaware of the terror already coiling around the eight visitors.

The sun withdrew its light beyond the jungle horizon. The full moon lifted its pale amber face to stare woefully through gray cloud fingers and spreading ironwood branches. The dancers clustered together under the treehouses, shouting unearthly minor cadences at the stars. The end of each cadence died out in a long, descending "ooooooooooooooo" while the drums maintained their steady beat.

Occasionally a sudden increase in the tempo of the drums would trigger a climax of wild exultant shouting. Out of the midst of each resounding tumult a single warrior would raise his voice to a high pitch and scream in rapid oratorical Sawi the details of a murder he had committed. The others would suddenly fall silent to listen.

The speaker would complete the story in five or six sentences, leaping straight up and down with spear poised, tossing his head from side to side. At the conclusion of his oration the entire assembly would break forth into shouting again, in commemoration of the slaying described. Then the drums would resume their ominous booming, portraying the long intervals of plotting and waiting which separate realizations of glorious treachery. Five, six or seven minutes later, the drums would trigger still another out-

burst of glory to conceive and bring to birth still another warrior's shrill boast of bloodthirstiness.

The chanting itself consisted entirely of nonsense syllables. The Sawi never used music to convey a message; they used it only to impress the senses. For them the medium was the message. The chains of colorful-sounding nonsense syllables were but one of several voice effects blended into the total pageant.

And so the chanters chanted while the starscape drifted and cooking fires gleamed red through cracks in sago-frond walls. The visitors ate merrily with their various hosts, enjoying compliments and hearty laughter, never dreaming that the real feast was to begin later, and that their own kinsman, Mahaen, had betrayed them to be the food for that feast.

Kani was the first to strike. He and Fusuman had climbed down to join the dancing for an hour or so. During a lapse in the chanting and drumbeating Kani had detected the echo of a *Haragu* bird's call, a sure signal that dawn was near. So he had invited Fusuman back up into his house to smoke tobacco.

Once Fusuman was comfortably seated and drawing deeply on the long bamboo pipe, Kani came up behind him in the darkness with a steel machete he had recently obtained in trade from a Kayagar. Kani tensed his muscles and struck a hard, deep blow to the base of Fusuman's skull. He had hoped the blow would at least paralyze his victim, if not kill him outright, but the machete was very dull. The Kayagar always kept the sharp ones for themselves.

Fusuman lurched forward, gagging. Kani reached for his other newly acquired possession, his steel axe.

Fusuman rolled over on his back and looked up at Kani looming over him in the flickering light.

"*Ave! Ave!* Older brother! Older brother!" he cried.

But Kani replied, "*No ke ave don nom! Ukeden!* Don't call me older brother! I am killing you!"

The axeblade struck again and again. The sound of it awoke Kani's two wives, but his children slept on. Kani's oldest wife Yae excitedly fanned her fire to life to see what had happened. She saw her husband bending over Fusuman in the act of beheading him. His legs were red with Fusuman's blood.

Kani laid Fusuman's head beside his corpse and quickly descended from his house. The drums were still throbbing, though somewhat more lazily. *Haragu* birds were sounding on all sides of the village now, as the first gray hint of dawn paled the east.

Kani ran to Maum's house and climbed up the ladder. Maum met him at the doorway. Kani whispered to him, "Have you killed yours yet?"

Maum scratched himself lazily and replied, "Not yet."

Kani said, "What are you waiting for? I've already beheaded mine."

Maum whistled a tiny birdcall of admiration and turned back into his house. Kani hurried back down the ladder. By the time he reached the ground he heard the thud of a spear and the strangled cries of Maum's victim, a man named Aidon. As Kani hurried on to Mavu's house, he did not notice Aidon scrambling down the same ladder he had just descended himself. By the time Maum found a second spear and started down after him, Aidon had vanished in the darkness, leaving only a trail of blood that would not be visible for another quarter hour.

Mavu, likewise, hearing of Kani's successful slaying, tried to kill his guest, Eseger, but only wounded him, being hindered by the presence of his own wives and children in the same house. Eseger fled bleeding into the night, the thunder of the drums masking his cries of warning to any of his friends who might still be alive.

Hani and Warahai managed to kill and behead their victim, a young man named Seg. Tausi and Mahaeri likewise were slain, while Iri and Meramer escaped with wounds.

The light of dawn revealed four headless victims laid out for butchering. The other four, by some superhuman effort of the will, managed to struggle homeward through miles of dense swamp and jungle, only to die from their wounds as they reached the stairpoles of their respective longhouses.

Through the weeks of celebration that followed, the people of Haenam fawned openly upon Kani and Mahaen. The fact that four of their eight victims had escaped beheading and cannibalization did not detract from the honor of the moment. What mattered, after all, was not the number of heads taken, but the quality of the treachery that secured them.

Together Kani and Mahaen had started a unique new legend on its way. Mainly through Kani's genius, they had given a vastly more daring expression to an ancient ideal of the Sawi people, an ideal which

unnumbered generations of their forebears had conceived, systematized and perfected over millenniums
of time. It was the ideal of using friendship to fatten
one's victims for the slaughter, of finding comfort
and delight in the misery and destruction of others.
It was the ideal symbolized inadvertently by the
occasional act of pillowing one's head on the skull
of a victim—even though the skulls of relatives were
more commonly used in this way, simply because
the skulls of cannibalized victims were too often
covered with black char from the cooking fires used
in their annihilation.

As every philosophy, once its basic tenets have been
accepted, draws it adherents irresistibly toward certain ultimate conclusions, so also the Sawi world view
had at last found what was possibly its ultimate
expression in the treachery of Kani and Mahaen.
Men, women and children now looked to them as
the epitome of Sawi manhood.

Their place in the sun, however, was about to be
challenged. And not only their place in the sun, but
also the very idealization of treachery which they
espoused was about to be engaged in something the
Sawi had never heard of before—a contest of values!

Kani and Mahaen were not yet aware that some
two thousand years earlier a supremely different kind
of Legendmaker had launched a new world view
based on love. It was a world view diametrically
opposed to the Sawi mind, as it was also to the minds
of millions who considered themselves much wiser
than people like the Sawi.

It had taken nearly two thousand years for the

message of that new value system to range from Galilee to the miasmal swamps of southwest New Guinea. On its way, that message had already challenged, engaged and conquered barbarity in many forms in the minds of millions of people, for it was an extremely *mettlesome* message. It was not cowed by earthly obstacles, for its strength was supernatural. It could not be intimidated, for it was itself the ultimate antidote to fear.

The message would not back away from any form of darkness, for it was light itself! It was not embarrassed if its bearers were sometimes plain, homely or even untaught—in fact it was fond of executing its most subtle strategies through such! To the consternation of its enemies, it could triumph even when its adherents were being decimated by sword or spear.

That message was the gospel of Jesus Christ. Its purpose was nonnegotiable—to persuade men from "every kindred, and tongue, and people and nation" to repent and be reconciled to God through Jesus Christ. That message was now about to invade the Sawi world, about to confront their idealization of treachery eye to eye in a relentless spiritual struggle for the souls of men, women and children. It would match prayer and preaching against spear and barbed arrow; faith and hope against systematized barbarity; love and compassion against entrenched fear and evil.

That invasion was about to be launched, that match to take place, that reconciliation to begin. For even now the first of the Legendmaker's message-bearers were about to come and dwell among the Sawi.

Part 2
When Worlds Meet

6

Genesis of a Mission

The angular seventy-one-year-old Englishman gripped the pulpit in his large bony hands and scrutinized the seven hundred students waiting in silence. His white hair was combed straight back. His spectacles rested halfway down the bridge of his nose. From under tufted brows his grey eyes shone with an intensity not yet dimmed by age.

Something in his presence seemed to transfix the assembly seated before him in the large auditorium. Three words rumbled, deep-voiced, from the old man's lips—three words weighted with his own unique blend of dignity and fervor:

"Netherlands New Guinea. . . ."

With those three words Ebenezer G. Vine, secretary of the Philadelphia council of an international mission society called the Regions Beyond Missionary Union, introduced his subject.[1] The year was 1955. His audience was the student body of the Prairie Bible Institute, a sprawling campus located on the wintry plains of Alberta, Canada, adjacent to a small town named Three Hills. Behind him L. E. Maxwell, the noted principal of this partially self-supporting Christian community and missionary training school, leaned forward in his chair. Equally white-haired, with a set jaw and determined countenance, he epitomized the rugged idealism of the school.

Mr. Vine felt a strong sense of purpose as he addressed this particular student body. Other campuses on his itinerary might boast more scholarly, more polished graduates than he would find here, where the motto was plainly and unaffectedly *training disciplined soldiers for Christ!* But even as he sounded the call for Christian pioneers to plant the banner of the gospel among isolated and potentially hostile stone-age tribes in interior Netherlands New Guinea, Mr. Vine knew it was not primarily scholarship and polish that would be required, though these were by no means excluded! Unwavering faith, self-denial, and an intimate communion with God were the crucial qualities that must be present, and these were the main qualities which "Prairie's" faculty and staff, both by example and life-centered biblical instruction, strove to impart to its students.

Mr. Vine knew well the story of Prairie's growth. Since its inception in a farmhouse with eight students in 1922, it had grown to be the largest Christian training institution in Canada. Because of its strong emphasis on foreign missions, already more than eleven hundred of its three thousand graduates had entered foreign missionary service, while hundreds of others were active as pastors and Christian workers in their home countries. On this basis, Mr. Vine knew that approximately 35 percent of the students before him would find their way to foreign fields under various mission societies. The Christless tribes of Netherlands New Guinea desperately needed some of them, he reasoned, as with great force and inner burden of heart he described the land and its violent, unpredictable people.

"Netherlands New Guinea," he continued, "is the western half of a 1400-mile-long island stretched along the edge of the Pacific Ocean north of Australia. It lies in the torrid zone, just south of the equator, yet within its vast watery area of 110,000 square miles, you will in some areas find yourself facing jagged mountain ranges hoary with ice at altitudes of more than fifteen thousand feet. In other areas, you may find yourself entangled in miasmal lowlands, where torrential rains combine with sweltering heat to sustain an enervating humidity.

"You may be called upon to make the first advance into the midst of entire tribes that have never known any kind of governmental control, where people are a law unto themselves and where savagery is a way of life. You must learn to make yourself and your message understood in the medium of languages never before learned by any outsider. There will be no dictionaries, grammars or primers to help you—you must produce your own.

"You will encounter customs and beliefs which will baffle you, but which must be understood if you are to succeed. You will try to treat loathsome tropical diseases and run the risk of being blamed for the death of your patient if you fail. You must prepare to endure loneliness, weariness and frustration with fortitude. Most of all, you must be prepared, in the strength of the Lord, to do battle with the prince of darkness, who, having held these hundreds of tribes captive these many thousands of years, is not about to give them up without a fight!"

The old man paused, and silence hung heavy under the great, arched ceiling of the auditorium.

"It was seven years ago," he continued, reminiscing, "that Paul Gesswein, a serviceman returned from the New Guinea war theater, approached me on this very campus and said, 'Mr. Vine, I have two questions to ask you. The first is, does the Regions Beyond Missionary Union realize there are tens of thousands of tribespeople isolated without the gospel in the interior of Netherlands New Guinea?'

"I said to him, 'How do you know they are there?'

"He replied, 'A military aircraft was missing on a flight over the interior. I took part in the search operations. As we flew over many uncharted areas of the interior, we were amazed to find valley after valley dotted with villages surrounded by extensive garden areas.'

"I said to him, 'What is your second question?'

"He replied, 'Will the Regions Beyond Missionary Union help me take the gospel to those people?'

"Awed by all that a positive answer to his question would entail, I first informed him we were already heavily committed to five fields—India, Nepal, Congo,

89

Peru and Borneo—and then, caught up in the excitement of it all, I added, 'I'll see what I can do!'

"Not many months later, after much prayer and deliberation, I had the pleasure of writing Paul Gesswein to say: 'RBMU Council has given approval! We are making application to the Netherlands government for permission to enter the interior of Netherlands New Guinea!'

"We soon found, however, that the Netherlands government rejected our request, arguing that their law enforcement agencies could not accept the responsibility of protecting our missionaries from the cannibals! We kept applying again and again. Eventually I even made three trips across the Atlantic to plead our request in person at the Hague! Only recently has the necessary permission been given.

"Now the way is open to the interior! Missionary Aviation Fellowship of California has already put one single-engine aircraft into operation flying men and supplies for our own and other missions into a major base camp called Bokondini, deep in the interior highlands. Paul Gesswein and our other volunteer, Bill Widbin, have already assisted in establishing Bokondini and are now preparing an advance over the mountains to a people called the Black Valley Danis. Their wives, meanwhile, are helping with logistics on the north coast until they can safely join their husbands."

At this point the speaker extended his right hand toward the students and continued:

"I cannot believe that God has brought RBMU to this great new threshold in order that two men and their wives should cross it alone! There must be others whom God will call to join them! There may be some such seated here before me now! If God has set you aside for this special task, not to build on another man's foundation, but to preach Christ where the sound of His name has not once fallen upon the ears of men, then RBMU will prayerfully consider your qualifications.

"How much longer must those lost tribes wait to hear of Him who died for their salvation and rose again nearly two thousand years ago? For the past one hundred years the messengers of Christ have been content to occupy only the accessible areas of the coastal fringe. Now new marching orders have come—*to the interior!*

"Our Lord is impatient to establish His kingdom of love in those dark places which are now the habitation of cruelty. Two men and their wives have gone ahead to establish a beachhead, and they are listening eagerly for word of reinforcements. Who will go and help them enlarge that beachhead?"

It was enough. God did not intend to frustrate the vision He had given to the elderly mission leader. One of the young men listening was Bill Mallon. Less than three years later, Bill and his wife, Barbara, joined Paul and Joy Gesswein and Bill and Mary Widbin among the Black Valley Danis. For four years Bill studied the Dani language, helping to discover the secrets of its grammar and preparing language lesson material for others who would follow.

In another part of the auditorium David Martin, the youngest member of his class, felt the finger of

God touching his own life, as did Margaret Colton, who later became David's wife. Together with Bill and Barbara Mallon, they later beheld thousands of Black Valley Dani warriors burning their fetishes and weapons of war in response to the message of the gospel.

To one side a young immigrant from Holland listened eagerly. He was John Dekker, who later with his wife, Helen, led a new advance into a branch of the Black Valley called Kanggime, which in Dani means "the place of death." Under their ministry the "place of death" abounded with new life as thousands of the inhabitants received Christ into their hearts.

Also two young single women, Judith Eckles and Winifred Frost, began to sense that their destinies were somehow related to what the speaker was saying. Within a few years they also joined the RBMU team in the Black Valley, teaching, healing, and counseling as the Dani church came to birth and began to grow before their eyes.

Elsewhere in the auditorium a young couple from rural Iowa listened intently—Philip and Phyliss Masters. They too soon shared in the limitless opportunities of ministry in the Black Valley and then pressed on to open Korupun among the testy Kimyal people. Thirteen years later, Phil Masters died on the bank of the Seng River, his body pierced by a hundred arrows of the Yali tribe, while Phyliss, his widow, through the comfort of the Holy Spirit, returned to the Black Valley with her five children to continue her ministry there.

There was also Richard Hale, who later, with his

wife, Wanda, ministered for three years in the Solomon Islands before reaching Netherlands New Guinea, where health problems cut short their ministry after one year.

In addition to these, other volunteers from Christian campuses in North America, England, Germany, and Australia soon joined hands to swell the ranks of RBMU's task force of career missionaries in Netherlands New Guinea to more than thirty by 1965. By that time the lives of some fourteen thousand stone-age Papuans were already deeply transformed by their ministry of preaching, teaching and healing.

Five years later, in 1971, the total number of adherents climbed to twenty-one thousand as a still larger missionary band joined forces with 176 newly-trained tribal Christian leaders to establish more than one hundred congregations and numerous schools and clinics in high mountain valleys and across lowland swamps.

Entire populations found dramatic release from an agelong oppression of savagery and superstition. They began to enjoy not only the blessings of spiritual wholeness through the gospel, but also of social peace and security such as they had never known. Education came in to fortify them against ruthless exploiters who might otherwise take advantage of their simplicity, as has so often happened to unprepared primitive peoples in other parts of the world.

Doctors and nurses operating from bush hospitals and clinics soon eradicated the terrible scourge of yaws and also helped to stem the severe epidemics of influenza, measles and whooping cough which for so long ravaged these tribes in their isolated state. In the midst of it all, the missionaries found themselves at times almost overwhelmed by the sheer intensity of the gratitude expressed by thousands who knew, better than any outsider could ever appreciate, how greatly their lives had been transformed by their acceptance of the gospel.

All of this, of course, did not come about without a great deal of work! Over the years, hundreds of thousands of missionary man-hours were invested in discovering the hidden rules of tribal languages, compiling dictionaries, inventing alphabets for previously unwritten languages; building houses, schools and clinics; carving out airstrips in jungle-covered terrain; trekking over cold mountain ridges; exploring serpentine rivers; probing the customs and beliefs of exotic tribes; preaching to thousands and teaching those who respond to read and write; translating the Scriptures; healing the sick and binding their sores; arbitrating between warring factions; hiring, supervising and paying workers; repairing generators, washing machines, outboard motors and tape recorders; maintaining correspondence with supporters in the homelands; keeping financial records; encouraging the despondent; pacifying the enraged; comforting the bereaved; entertaining visitors; ordering supplies months in advance; praying for needed funds; and thanking God for the fantastic privilege of sharing in it all!

All that can be said of the ministry of the Regions Beyond Missionary Union (RBMU) can be repeated concerning the work of the Unevangelized Fields

Mission (UFM), The Evangelical Alliance Mission (TEAM), the Asia and Pacific Christian Mission (APCM), the Christian and Missionary Alliance (C&MA), the Australian Baptist Mission Society (ABMS), and the Missionary Aviation Fellowship (MAF). The resourceful flying ministry of the MAF enables the other six missions to maintain adequate logistics while crossing the formidable swamp and mountain barriers of the land. West New Guinea soon grew to become MAF's largest field of operations, requiring the full-time use of as many as eight single-engine and two twin-engine aircraft.

Gesswein, Vine and other pioneers of this new frontier estimated the population of the interior in terms of tens of thousands. In actual fact, close to 300,000 "stone-agers" would be discovered even before all areas were fully explored! The six church-planting missions, supported by the flying services of MAF, by the sum of their respective ministries, saw about 125,000 of these nearly 300,000 individuals express their own personal adherence to the Christian faith before the end of 1971.

Many of these converts matched, if not actually surpassed, the faith and devotion of the missionaries themselves. Some of them, like Yali Christians Bingguok and Yeikwarahu, suffered martyrdom, triumphant and uncomplaining, calling upon their murderers to receive Christ. Stan Dale, an RBMU missionary from Australia, sustained five arrow wounds trying to rescue them.

Two years later Stan himself died beside Philip Masters in a further uprising of the Yali people.

Within a few months after their martyrdom, the attitude of the hostile Yali people began to change. Soon dozens of villages welcomed Christian evangelists from the Black Valley Dani church. Still later hundreds began to turn to Christ, including many of the murderers of the four martyrs.

But all of this, of course, was still hidden in the mystery of the future back in 1955 when Ebenezer Vine unburdened his soul before the student body of the Prairie Bible Institute. Nevertheless, as one of the seven hundred students listening that day, it seemed to me that God had suddenly come among us with a plan, looking for the people He would use to make that plan come to fruition.

I also had the unmistakable feeling that I was one of those He was scrutinizing. With that feeling strongly upon me, I returned from the chapel service to my room in the dormitory. I could hardly wait to get alone before God in prayer and ask, "Is this it? Is this what You want me to do?"

I was twenty years old at the time. Three years earlier I had experienced for the first time the new life, the love, the joy of knowing Jesus Christ in a personal way. A crisis came, I called upon Him, and suddenly He was there, alive! In fact, two thousand years had not aged Him a bit! I found He still had the same power to transform men's lives and hold their loyalty that He had manifested in the Gospels two millenniums before.

Now the old, threadbare, archaic-sounding chapters and verses began to explode with new meaning, as God gave me a heart to understand what they had been saying all along. With Christ at its center, the universe began to make sense. By serving Him, life could have eternal meaning. Knowing Him and sharing Him with others would henceforth be my consuming purpose! And if sharing Him where His name was already known was a privilege, sharing Him where His name had never been heard must be an immeasurably greater privilege!

With these thoughts in mind, I had begun to study the map of the world. I also began to search for a Christian campus which could impart to me the kind of biblical knowledge and spirit I would need to communicate Christ effectively to men and women of another culture. Guided by the peace of God, I had enrolled at the Prairie Bible Institute in the fall of 1953.

There the dynamic teaching, the fellowship with other students of like purpose, and the exposure to visiting missionary speakers from almost every part of the world, served to confirm still more deeply the conviction that God was calling me to serve Him abroad. Still, there were so many options, so many fields pleading for workers, so many needy people waiting for a chance to hear. Thus the question loomed ever larger: where in this great, wide world does God want me to serve Him?

For three years, the answer had eluded me. At last, in 1955, as I pondered Ebenezer Vine's message, my heart had begun to pound as an inner voice seemed to say, "This is it!" Both the call and my resolution to follow it would be severely tested. Disappointments and delays would at times seem to block the way, but still that call would remain, beckoning, drawing.

Still another Prairie Bible Institute student who was present when Ebenezer Vine delivered that stirring call to Netherlands New Guinea was lovely, blond Carol Soderstrom from Cincinnati, Ohio. First separately and later together we began to pursue the opportunity of serving God with RBMU in New Guinea. For three years after graduating from Prairie, Carol trained as a nurse while I gained further experience as a pastor and a youth worker.

Then in August 1960, we were united in marriage. The following summer found us both attending a linguistic course offered by the Summer Institute of Linguistics at the University of Washington in Seattle. In November of 1961 our first child, Stephen, was born. Soon afterwards our visas to Netherlands New Guinea were granted. We sailed from Vancouver on the *Oriana* on March 19, 1962, and on April 13 arrived at Sentani, an airfield on the north coast of Netherlands New Guinea. Seven days later MAF pilot Dave Steiger took us on our first flight into the interior. We landed at Karubaga, RBMU's main station in the Black Valley.

Here we saw nearly naked tribesmen sporting stone axes, and string-skirted women digging with wooden sticks in their sweet potato gardens. Surrounded by hundreds of the Dani people, Philip and Phyliss Masters, former classmates David and Margaret Martin and Winnie Frost, and other RBMU colleagues welcomed us at the airstrip.

After greetings and introductions, David Martin and I walked out across the countryside while he explained to me much concerning the culture of the Dani people and the brief history of RBMU's work among them. Eventually we came to the subject of what part Carol and I might expect to have in the future of this work.

David stopped and gazed out across the grassy Karubaga plateau to the mountainsides dotted with Dani villages. "There is still much to be done here in the Black Valley, but in our recent field conference we had a great deal of discussion about the needs of other tribes that are still unreached. In fact, we have already entered into an agreement with TEAM giving us responsibility for a large area of the vast swampy plain that extends from the southern slopes of these ranges to the shores of the Arafura Sea.

"John and Glenna McCain from Florida have already gone down to that area. For five months they have been working among a people called the Kayagar. From their reports, the area is anything but hospitable. Many of the tribes in that region are still practicing both cannibalism and headhunting and are generally not to be trusted. And the climate is as hot, humid, and unhealthy as it can possibly be.

"Nevertheless we agreed to ask you and Carol to consider the area. We realize you may have apprehensions about taking little Stephen down to a place like that, and if you would rather work somewhere else, feel free to say so. But if God gives you peace about going to one of the other tribes in our southern area of responsibility, the way is open for you."

After two days of waiting upon God in prayer, we gave David Martin our answer. "Yes, we are happy to go to one of the tribes in the south! How soon can we leave?"

On May 19 MAF pilot Hank Worthington flew us from Karubaga to the southern lowlands. We watched in awe as the mighty ranges in the area of Mount Wilhelmina suddenly dropped from altitudes of more than fifteen thousand feet down to sea level. Ahead of us shimmering, emerald swamps, veined with turgid streams, lush with endless sago thickets, stretched as far as the eye could see. Somewhere in the midst of it we were to build a home and live in the midst of a cannibal-headhunter tribe.

At last the coastline of the Arafura Sea swam into view as Hank Worthington nosed the Cessna toward our destination, a tiny Dutch government outpost called Pirimapun. There TEAM missionaries, Dr. Ken Dresser and his wife, Sylvia, had established a new beachhead among the southern Asmat people. Our RBMU colleagues, John and Glenna McCain, were also there. They had journeyed out of the swamps in their 26-foot riverboat to meet us and take us with them to their home among the Kayagar.

That afternoon as the six of us sipped a cool drink in the living room of the Dresser's prefabricated aluminum home, Carol and I were able to become better acquainted with these two resourceful couples who had preceded us to this "uttermost part of the earth." John and Glenna were no strangers to swamp country, having grown up near the Everglades along Florida's western coast. A quiet, determined couple, they were deeply dedicated to the task of bringing Christ to the Kayagar people, who had already sent one missionary couple home with broken health.

Ken Dresser, an ingenious Canadian physician, had already faced difficulties and frustrations that many would have considered insurmountable. And he knew he would face many more, yet his calm eyes radiated a peace and contentment that never seemed to leave him. His wife Sylvia shared his fortitude, laboring cheerfully beside her husband in the operating room of their bush hospital and caring for her home and children. Many years would pass before the Asmat people would begin to show a genuine response to their ministry of spiritual and physical kindness.

During the course of the conversation, Ken Dresser acquainted us with the history of this remote location. Nearly two hundred years earlier British Captain James Cook had anchored his ship near this very point and sent a lorry ashore to search for fresh water. Yet as far as Dr. Dresser could determine, the Asmat people retained no memory of the history-making event!

They told us of the recent tragic and mysterious disappearance of Michael Rockefeller, son of the former Governor of New York State, at a point just twenty-two miles north of the Dresser's home and only seven months earlier. And both the McCains and the Dressers spoke intensely and informatively of their own interesting experiences among the Kayagar and Asmat people.

At length I questioned John McCain as to which of the other tribes in RBMU's area of responsibility he judged Carol and I should enter. John replied, "After giving thought to all the factors involved,

Glenna and I both recommend you go to the tribe living to the northwest of our Kayagar people, the tribe called the Sawi."

After years of preparing and waiting, just to hear the name of the people we would devote our lives to was exciting! The Sawi! I turned the name over in my mind. I could almost taste its savor on the tip of my tongue. It had the same tang of inscrutable mystery that pervaded even the very jungle outside the Dresser's back door.

The next morning we said good-bye to the Dressers and left Pirimapun, following the bends of the Cook River toward John and Glenna's home in the Kayagar village called Kawem, forty miles deep in the sago swamps.

FOOTNOTES

1. Regions Beyond Missionary Union, 8102 Elberon Avenue, Philadelphia, Pennsylvania 19111.

7

Through the Ironwood Curtain

John McCain's 26-foot river launch, the *Ebenezer* (named for Ebenezer Vine), rolled easily at the dock as we loaded fuel and supplies in the predawn darkness. Nearby, the friendly light of kerosene lamps gleamed inside the McCain's Kingstrand aluminum home, where Glenna and Carol were packing food supplies for our journey. Further away, the black shapes of Kayagar longhouses hulked in two long rows beside the starlit path of the Cook River.

By 5:30 A.M. we were underway. The launch's Volkswagen engine roared to life, and John pointed her prow downstream. Our wives waved good-bye from the dock. Carol was holding baby Stephen, who had just awakened. His tiny face was barely visible in the pale blue of early dawn as he snuggled close to Carol's blond hair. Beside them stood Herep, the Kayagar headman who in the past had proved to be a faithful protector of John's family and property whenever John had had to leave them in this isolated outpost. A second protector was the McCain's fierce watchdog, Patches. In addition, a radio transmitter in the McCain's home would enable the two women to call for help if trouble developed.

The full light of dawn found us threading the narrow channel of the Cook westward toward Pirimapun. Around us a shimmering panorama of emerald grasslands, graceful palms and dense sago thickets formed a vast, windswept concourse for the swarms of snowy egrets, pastel ducks, and black-throated geese constantly flushed into the sky by our passing. Still higher overhead, spectral hordes of giant fruit bats drifted unveeringly southward as if controlled by a single sinister mind. Weary from a night of foraging under the stars, they would soon hide their freakish heads inside the voluminous, leathery membranes of their wings to sleep out the day, hanging by the thousands in some distant thicket of the jungle.

Four hours later we reached Pirimapun, where TEAM's Dr. Ken Dresser was waiting to join us in our attempt to contact the Sawi tribe. We took his fiberglass skiff and outboard motor in tow, in case the *Ebenezer* developed engine trouble in some remote sector of the wilderness. Leaving Pirimapun, we veered north across the Arafura Sea, looking for the mouths of rivers that would lead us back into Sawi territory.

Three days later the *Ebenezer* turned into the mouth of the Kronkel and began to follow the same tortuous course the Dutch riverboats had followed approximately two years earlier. In the intervening period we had explored the Au River and contacted three Sawi villages named Mauro, Hahami and Ero. In all three villages, women and children had fled into the jungle at our approach, but some of the men remained to meet us on the shore. I was able to elicit a number of Sawi words from these brief encounters, a small start on a language that probably contained several thousand terms.

In a fourth village, Sato, the treehouses stood empty at our approach, all inhabitants having fled in terror. I climbed up into one of the treehouses and left a small gift in the center of the floor, as an indication of good will. Later we learned we had missed two other villages, Mosi and Tamor, because they were hidden deep in the recesses of the jungle. But we had ascertained the existence of a sizable Sawi population along the Au River.

Now we hoped to find an even larger population along the Kronkel. Following the switchbends of the Kronkel quickly used up the remaining hours of daylight, so after we had passed a safe distance beyond the two large Asmat villages situated in the lower part of the river, we dropped anchor in the middle of the channel and cooked our evening meal.

Next morning we decided to leave the slower *Ebenezer* at anchor and make a quick strike toward the headwaters of the river in Ken Dresser's sixteen-foot skiff. Cutting the bends at about twenty-five knots we quickly left the Asmat region far behind and soon saw a few scant evidences of Sawi population in the form of abandoned treehouses rotting on their stilts.

Presently we passed the mouth of the Hanai tributary, which led back to the hideaway where, still unknown to us, Haenam had killed and devoured the four men from Wasohwi a few months earlier. Swinging north around a sharp bend we came to the old village site where the two Dutch riverboats had startled Haenam and Kamur two years before. It was now so overgrown with trees that we hardly noticed it.

Next the long expanse of the straight stretch of river, which I later learned was called the *kidari,* opened up before us. I remarked to John McCain, "This stretch of river would make an excellent landing site for the MAF float plane."

At the far end of the *kidari* we discovered more rotting treehouses of still another abandoned village. We knew that if we pressed on much further we would enter Kayagar territory, so we beached the skiff at the abandoned village site, right where another tributary flowed into the Kronkel from the north. We stepped ashore onto the same knoll of high ground where Kigo, Hato and Numu, two years earlier, had come out into the open and faced the advancing riverboats in an act of monumental courage.

But there was no one to welcome us now. The brooding jungle stood tall against the sky, walling in the overgrown clearing as if to create an arena for an impending contest. I listened to the wind soughing through the derelict structures, rustling the smoke-blackened, rotting thatch. I watched a fish cleave the limpid surface of the quiet, tree-shadowed tributary.

The wildness of the locale seemed to taunt me. Something in the mood of the place seemed to say mockingly, "I am not like your tame, manageable Canadian homeland. I am tangled. I am too dense to walk through. I am hot and steamy and drenched with rain. I am hip-deep mud and six-inch sago thorns. I am death adders and taipans and leeches and crocodiles. I am malaria and dysentery and filariasis and hepatitis.

"Your idealism means nothing here. Your Christian gospel has never scrupled the conscience of my children. You think you love them, but wait until you know them, if you *can* ever know them! You presume you are ready to grapple with me, understand my mysteries and change my nature. But I am easily able to overpower you with my gloom, my remoteness, my heedless brutality, my indolence, my unashamed morbidity, my total *otherness!*

"Think again, before you commit yourself to certain disillusionment! Can't you see I am no place for your wife? I am no place for your son. I am no place for you. . . ."

The voices of the leafy arena seemed to swell and then fade back into the masses of creeping tendrils and twisted vines. I turned and looked back at John and Ken waiting by the skiff. Beyond them that appealingly straight stretch of river glimmered in the sun. The ground on which I stood seemed reasonably high. The rotting treehouses were evidence of population hidden in the jungle around us. The little tributary might prove to lead close to other centers of population further north.

It's only a bluff, I thought. This swamp also is part of my Father's creation. His providence can sustain us here as well as anywhere else. Then the peace of God descended on me and suddenly this strange place became home! My home! I turned to Ken and John and said, "This is where I want to build!"

They nodded in agreement. The die was now cast! And high overhead, a white cockatoo glided up onto a girder-like limb of an ironwood tree and cocked his head at the unaccustomed sight of three clothed strangers and a skiff. Unfurling his yellow crest, he promptly swooped down again and away, shrieking as if to warn the jungle that its bluff had been called.

But deep among the vines and tendrils a young man named Seg crouched, watching our movements apprehensively. Then as we embarked again in the skiff, Seg turned and hurried away into the shadowed vaults of the forest to warn the village called Kamur of our presence.

Before returning to the *Ebenezer* we proceeded further upstream in search of still other signs of Sawi population. But here again we found only rotting houses or overgrown village sites.

Then we met two Kayagar men in a dugout. They recognized John McCain from visits they had made to the Cook River area. With his knowledge of the Kayagar language, John was able to learn from them that there were no other Sawi villages located upstream. We discovered also that the abandoned village we had just left was called Kamur. They advised us also that Kamur had recently relocated near the source of the tributary we had seen.

We requested them to guide us to the new site of Kamur. They hesitated, but when we offered them payment, they agreed. We told them to sit down in their canoe and then threw a rope around its pointed prow. Ken started up the Johnson outboard motor, and soon we were racing back downstream with two wide-eyed Kayagar hanging on for dear life to the sides of their little craft.

When we reached the mouth of the tributary, the tide had dropped, revealing masses of fallen trees nearly blocking the channel. It was obvious the skiff could never navigate in such a tangle of logs, but we thought the Kayagar's small craft might be light enough to skim over most of the barriers. John and I fitted ourselves precariously into the narrow canoe and started up the tributary while Ken stayed by the skiff. Before we had proceeded a hundred yards it became clear, however, that even the Kayagar craft could not find enough water to float, so we abandoned the attempt and returned to Ken and the skiff on the main river.

After paying the two Kayagar for their help, we started back downstream toward the *Ebenezer*. We were disappointed at not having made contact with a single Sawi person on the Kronkel River. But, our disappointment was to be short-lived!

Kani and thirty-nine others warriors from Haenam and Yohwi villages warily needled their black dugouts through the winding, vegetation-walled tunnel which was the course of the Hanai tributary. Packs of fresh sago flour and toasted beetle grubs filled the spaces between the feet of the paddlers. A number of lori parrots fluttered on the end of their tethers like little bursts of red, blue and green color. Native chickens likewise looked out over the sago packs.

The forty men were embarking on a new kind of adventure—a trading journey to the new government outpost called Pirimapun. For almost two years they had been hearing fabulous stories about Pirimapun from the Kayagar and from Atohwaem villages along the Cook River. Many times they had almost worked up enough courage to make the dread journey, but fear had restrained them. Now it was do or die!

On the previous day they had hidden their women-folk and children and their valuable possessions deep in the jungle in the care of the older men of the village. Then just after sunrise they had rendezvoused near the source of the Hanai tributary where their four new canoes were ready. Now they were approaching the mouth of the Hanai at the end of the first leg of their journey.

Kani crouched down on the sleek tip of the lead canoe, and peered out through screening branches at the bright expanse of the Kronkel. It would be fatal to burst out into the open and find oneself face to face with a flotilla of Asmat war canoes. The Kronkel was clear, so Kani struck his paddle deep and moved out into the open. The other paddlers followed suit.

With the tips of their spear-paddles scissoring over their heads, they turned upstream toward the Kayagar area, taking the long way to Pirimapun in order to avoid the still hostile Asmat villages who guarded the lower Kronkel. They knew it was possible to reach the Cook River by cutting through the flooded Kayagar grasslands, and the Kayagar recently had become increasingly friendly toward their former enemies, the Sawi. The travelers were not expecting any trouble from the Kayagar, but just in case, the inside walls of their canoes were lined with forty palmwood bows and hundreds of barb-tipped arrows.

The adventurers had already committed themselves to the long expanse of the *kidari* when suddenly their newly mustered courage was tested to the limit. Straight ahead of them, and just out of sight around the bend at the far end of the *kidari,* a strange sound like the whine of an angry hornet split the quiet of the morning. It grew rapidly louder, droning straight toward them!

Suddenly a pale yellow craft darted into sight, streamers of spray flaring behind it. In the craft were three figures covered in bright-colored skins. Tuans! Pandemonium broke loose in the four canoes.

As we turned into the *kidari,* Ken suddenly pointed straight ahead. Turning, we saw four canoes full of men who could only be Sawi. My heart stirred within me at the sight of them.

The appearance of our skiff had thrown them into complete disorder. Some leaped from their canoes and plunged in among the reeds, while others waved their paddles frantically trying to maintain their bal-

ance in the confusion. Those who remained in their canoes had no time to flee.

Within a few seconds we were drawing up beside them and John was calling to them in Kayagar, encouraging them not to be afraid. Among them was the Atohwaem warrior, Hadi, who was fluent in both Kayagar and Sawi as well as his own mother tongue. Hearing John's words of reassurance, Hadi quickly translated them into Sawi with a clear, ringing voice, easily heard above the confused uproar of forty disquieted warriors.

All were lithe, wiry, hard-muscled men, naked except for their armbands and ornaments. Most of them were actually trembling, which caused their fragile dugout canoes to tremble with them. The canoes in turn made the dark surface of the Kronkel shiver in resonance with the feelings of the forty, giving the impression that the men, their canoes and nature were all in harmony.

Drawing our skiff alongside one of the canoes, we touched fingertips with the nearest warriors, using the Sawi greeting, *"Konahario!"* which had worked so well in the villages we had visited on the Au River. Hearing it, these men of the Kronkel also responded exuberantly. To release their nervous tension they shouted *"Konahario!"* back at us so loudly as to be almost unnerving.

One by one, those who had hidden themselves among the reeds swam out of hiding and climbed back into their canoes. We then passed out a dozen or more empty tin cans which we had saved for such an occasion. They quickly snapped them up. Tin cans are highly prized by these people whose only water containers were lengths of hollow bamboo. Not one of those tin cans would fall as litter in the jungle. They would be used and re-used until they rusted away.

John then learned from Hadi that the expedition was bound for Pirimapun. Ken Dresser exclaimed, "This is a big adventure for them! It will probably be the first time in their history that they have ventured outside their own territory to meet with civilization. And God has providentially timed our survey to meet them in the first few miles of their journey!" Ken was right, for if we had started on our return journey a few minutes earlier, we would have passed the mouth of the Hanai before the expedition emerged from it.

Our attention was drawn, not to men like Kani, Mahaen, and Maum, but to Hadi. His bright personality and apparent fearlessness, plus his facility as an interpreter, persuaded us that he would be a valuable help in my future contacts with the Sawi. John invited him to make the journey with us by outboard back to the *Ebenezer* and then to Pirimapun and Kawem, where he could join the party of travelers again on the morrow. During the journey I would have time to establish personal rapport with him and perhaps learn more of the Sawi language as well.

Hearing our invitation, Hadi, in spite of his dark skin, turned pale! We could almost see his stomach churning under his tense skin as he weighed the implications of our offer. To accept would not only mean committing his life to the uncertain mercy of

114

three bizarre and possibly nonhuman aliens. It would also mean traveling with them into the dread region of the fiendish Asmat cannibals. If he made it past the Asmat, he would still have to brave traveling on the ocean, an experience completely beyond his ken.

Although Hadi had lived all his life only twenty air miles from the Arafura Sea, he had never once laid eyes upon it. He had, however, heard several awe-inspiring second- or third-hand reports of what it was like. Often during the season of westerly monsoon storms, he had heard the distant thunder of thousands of mighty breakers pounding night and day on the Arafura mud flats and trembled to think how terrible it would be if one were close to the source of that formidable sound!

On the other hand, what an adventure the journey would be! And how great would be his prestige among his people if he returned safely! The story of his odyssey would enthrall at least three tribes, for Hadi could speak three languages! His journey would mark a major turning point in the history of his people, for he would learn much about the Tuans which would prepare the way for future contacts with them.

The potential benefits, Hadi decided, outweighed the potential dangers. "I'll go with you!" he said to John, tremblingly. We rejoiced, while Hadi's friends stared at him with evident concern for his safety. They had not yet had time to make the same evaluation Hadi had made.

John then wisely decided to invite a second person to accompany Hadi, to help allay pangs of misgiving or loneliness which he might feel during the journey.

The one chosen was a smiling youth named Er (bird). Following the lead of Hadi, who was his elder, Er courageously accepted our offer.

We took them both on board, hopefully assuring the other wayfarers that they would find Hadi and Er well and happy at Kawem when they passed that way on the morrow. Then with a final *"Konahario!"* we left them standing somewhat bewildered, gazing after us through the spray kicked up by the outboard motor. Within seconds we had left the *kidari* behind on our return journey to the Arafura Sea still forty winding river-miles away.

Thirty minutes later we found the *Ebenezer* just as we left it, tied the skiff to its stern, and resumed our seaward journey. Hadi, Er and I sat down on top of the cabin and I continued plying Hadi for more Sawi terminology, with help in the Kayagar language from John McCain, who stood below us at the wheel.

When at length we came within sight of the first Asmat village, Hadi and Er grew tense with fear. They could no longer concentrate on the questions I was asking, so I had to let the language study wait until we were well past the dreaded presence. The Asmat, a lean, hungry-looking people, simply lined up along the shore and stared blankly as the *Ebenezer* left its wake at their feet.

As we rounded the last bend of the Kronkel and faced the open sea, Hadi and Er gasped. Stretched like a taut wire between the mangrove swamps on

116

either side of the river mouth was the horizon line of the Arafura Sea. Burnished by the late afternoon sun, it gleamed so brightly it hurt our eyes to try to focus on it. To Hadi and Er it must have seemed that we were journeying into nothingness itself, as the *Ebenezer* boldly ventured far out toward that ever-receding, glittering seam of sky and sea, and then veered south toward Pirimapun.

Once the *Ebenezer* began to roll on the ocean swell, Hadi and Er gripped the handrails apprehensively, fearing the launch might capsize. I laid my hand on Hadi's shoulder and calmly whispered to him two Sawi words he himself had taught me a few hours earlier, *"Tadan nom!* Don't be afraid!"

Hadi looked at me, and slowly a smile of returning confidence brightened his countenance. He replied, *"Tadan haser!* I'm not afraid!" and let go of the handrail to prove it. Er followed suit.

Turning into the mouth of the Cook River at Pirimapun, Ken Dresser disengaged his skiff and took leave of us, while John and I pressed on through descending darkness, following the bends of the Cook by spotlight.

At one o'clock in the morning the familiar outline of the McCain's home stood out against the stars. Our first journey to the Sawi was ended. I stepped up onto the dock and felt Carol's welcoming arms enfold me in the darkness.

"Is everything all right?" I whispered in her ear.

"Just perfect!" she replied enthusiastically.

"Guess what—we have two Sawi on board!" I said, still not aware that Hadi belonged to the Atohwaem tribe.

I could feel a thrill of joy well up within her as she peeked curiously past my shoulder at the shadowy figures of Hadi and Er, barely visible in the glow of the *Ebenezer's* cabin light.

Once accommodations for Hadi and Er had been arranged, Carol and I stole quietly into the room where Stephen was sleeping in the screened cot John McCain had so carefully fashioned for him. Turning our flashlight close enough to reveal his rounded cheeks and wispy, golden hair, but not close enough to awaken him, we stood hand in hand and gazed wistfully upon this vision of cherubic serenity which was our son. Whatever destiny awaited us among the Sawi, Stephen would share it, for better or for worse. We were sure it would be for the better.

Our confidence in God was running at a high level and getting higher. Exhilarated with a buoyant spirit of trust, we never seriously considered that some dread disease of the swamps might steal the blush of health from our baby's cheeks, or that any other danger might seriously threaten any of us. "If God be for us, who can be against us!" was the watchword that uplifted us night and day.

It seemed, furthermore, that this bracing excitement was not our own, but was being communicated to us through the presence of God—as if God Himself had been waiting such a long, long time to do whatever He was going to do for the Sawi through us, and was delighted that at last the time had come!

It had never occurred to me before that God could feel *excited,* that the One who is omnipresent in time as well as space could actually, as it were, isolate part of His consciousness on a single world-line and anticipate the future as if He were not already experiencing it!

It's true, I thought—God is excited and we, like children, are getting excited along with our Parent's contagious joy! This intuition only served to heighten still further our eager expectation of whatever God was preparing for us and for the Sawi.

With earnest longing we pleaded with God that the message of redemption in Christ might quickly break through all barriers, satanic or cultural, and spread this blessed contagion of joy to those strange, fearful men we had encountered that morning on the Kronkel River. How long it would take, I could not even guess. I only knew my life would not be complete until it happened!

A shout went up at the far end of Kawem village. "The Sawi are coming!"

Hadi, Er and I broke off language work and walked out to the end of the McCain's dock. There they were! Four canoes advancing in single file, giving Kawem a wide berth by keeping close to the reedy north shore of the Cook. Hadi and Er raised their arms to catch their attention, and all four dugouts quickly veered straight toward us.

The thirty-eight paddlers seemed tense and brooding as they beached their canoes around the dock.

Now far from their own territory, they were feeling the strangeness of it all very keenly. And they still had another forty miles to paddle before they reached Pirimapun! Herep, the Kayagar headman, came running from Kawem and greeted the wayfarers. Two or three of them gave Herep several sticks festooned with toasted beetle grubs, a sort of safe passage fee.

By this time, Hadi and Er had agreed to stay with us at Kawem for further language work, and so the travelers continued on without them. Two days later they were back, having sold their wares in the "big city" of Pirimapun. Bone-weary and solemn after paddling forty miles upstream, they rested by sitting on their paddles or on the sides of their canoes, while Hadi and Er gathered together the goods we had paid them for four days of language work.

As Hadi and Er resumed their places in two of the dugouts, John McCain gave Hadi one last cryptic message before the four canoes departed. "You and your people should spend some time fishing on the Kronkel for a few days!"

Hadi smiled knowingly and translated the message to the Sawi. It meant they should keep lookouts posted for us, because we intended to return, but couldn't say exactly when it would be.

As yet we had said nothing to either Kayagar or Sawi about our intention to reside on the Kronkel, because of the intervillage or intertribal rivalries this news might engender if made known too early. For the Kayagar were quite determined that Carol and I should stay within their territory.

As the four canoes departed, Hadi and Er stood

looking back at us, waving—two enthusiastic, outgoing optimists in a crowd of grim, determined men. It had been easy to win the friendship of Hadi and Er, but what about the others?

It was too early yet to know what the underlying attitudes of the majority would prove to be. But we would soon find out.

8

The End of an Aeon

By 7 A.M. that day in June, 1962, the two Kayagar dugouts were loaded and the six paddlers ready. One dugout wobbled uncertainly under the weight of two empty 55-gallon steel drums. The other was neatly packed with a large mosquito net and bedroll, a week's supply of food, tools for building, and trade goods to pay workers. These were all loaned to me by the McCains, as our own equipment had not yet arrived from North America.

I kissed Carol and Stephen good-bye and embarked in the latter canoe, as Glenna handed me a container of boiled water for drinking and a lunch for midday. I thanked her as we pulled away from the shore, while John gave final instructions to the Kayagar paddlers.

Our plan was for me to take a shortcut by dugout through the swamps to the Kronkel River, renew contact with the Sawi, and begin construction of a temporary home, while John returned to Pirimapun with the *Ebenezer* to complete construction of a storage house we had been building there. Five or six days later, John planned to continue north along the coastline to the Kronkel River, and then follow the river up to join me in completing the temporary house on the Kronkel.

As we struck out across the flooded grasslands, the silence of the wilderness closed in upon us, disturbed only by the swish of paddles and the lisping voice of kunai grass caressing the dugouts. Overhead, occasional halos of sunlight gleamed through a brooding overcast, shedding a misty glow on the dense sago forests looming beyond the grasslands.

Soon we penetrated the sago thickets, and the watercourse rapidly grew narrower. For about two hours we followed a sharply twisting channel and then broke out onto the grasslands which drain into the Kronkel River. At this point three canoes crowded with boisterous Kayagar men intercepted us. Hemming us in on all sides, they bent down and gripped my arms, shouting loudly and pointing ahead.

They had obviously surmised by the kind of equipment I was transporting that I intended to build a home somewhere in the Kronkel area, and they were determined that it should be built at the site of their own village, Amyam.

They seemed to be saying something like, "Tuan, don't go to the Sawi! They kill and eat people! Come to our village! In our village there is lots of high ground. We will help you build a real good house! Come to our village! Come to our village! Come to our village!"

Their shouting swelled to a tumult as we floated on toward the Kronkel. I tried in vain to quench their hopes. Using my sparse vocabulary of Indonesian and Kayagar, I urged my own paddlers to explain to these strangers that I was heading for the Sawi village called Kamur. My paddlers, however, were clearly halfhearted in passing on my message.

I began to sense a conspiracy. The paddlers also were Kayagar, after all, and were not eager to see the Sawi obtain the steel axes, machetes, and other trade goods which I was sure to dispense over periods of time. I began to realize that a major campaign to pressure me into choosing the village of Amyam was building up around me.

John McCain had earlier warned that before long the people of the area would test my will to see if I could be intimidated, and that it was of the utmost importance that I pass the test, otherwise Carol and I would be swamped with troubles from then on, and would end up broken in health or discouraged. So this is it, I thought, and steeled my will.

For another two hours the shouting and the pressure continued. Still other canoes joined our entourage, swelling the tumult. Unable to reason with them in any language they could understand, I simply sat quietly, waiting. Unfortunately, they took my silence for submission, and began exulting and shouting in unison, proclaiming far and wide that fortune had smiled upon them and given them a Tuan of their own to make them all rich.

Then I looked up and saw what must be the village of Amyam straight ahead. The Kayagar in the canoes around me now began to thump their paddle blades on the sides of their canoes to announce the triumphal arrival of Amyam's Tuan to his splendid new capital city! As we came abreast of the village, my paddlers looked at me enquiringly, pointing to Amyam and urging that we stop there.

I said determinedly in mixed Kayagar and Indonesian, *"Sevi terus ke Kamur!* Go straight on to Kamur!"

Dejectedly, they resumed paddling, and then it happened! A large, swift Kayagar dugout came rushing from the right-hand side, curving in front of us and forcing our canoe over to the shore in front of the village. Meanwhile people from the village itself came running, calling to me, waving, beckoning, pleading.

I hated to disappoint them, but straining every muscle to keep my balance in the narrow dugout, I rose to my feet, towered up to my full six-foot-two, and roared, "GO STRAIGHT ON TO KAMUR!!!"

Silence fell. For a few seconds it was not clear whether they would accept my demand or react with bitter resentment. Then, very sulkily, the men in the dugout which was barring our way moved it aside. We slowly paddled back into midstream and continued our journey.

I had passed the first test, yet I felt very sad, as a messenger of Christ, to have to refuse such a hearty invitation from so needy a people. Yet I knew that Amyam would later hear the gospel in their own language from the lips of John McCain, and this fact made their need less pressing than that of the Sawi, who still had no messenger who could speak to them in their own tongue. Still, Amyam earned a special place in my heart that day, and through the years I would pray for them more earnestly than for any other Kayagar village.

Borne along by the Kronkel's steady current, we passed quickly through a region which in more troubled times had been the no-man's-land separating the Kayagar and Sawi tribes. As we entered Sawi territory, my Kayagar paddlers pointed to various tributaries emptying into the Kronkel, and cited the names of Sawi villages which could be reached by following each of those tributaries to their sources in the sago swamps.

One such tributary was called the Sumdu. "It leads to Wiar," they informed me. Next on the left, they said, was the Baitom, which leads to Hadi's village, called Yohwi.

"Hadi's village?" I repeated. "Quick! Turn in to the Baitom and take me to Hadi. I want to see him before we go on to Kamur."

We turned into the shadowed course of the Baitom and followed it for about a mile into the thickening jungle. Suddenly we broke through into a clearing and saw six longhouses ranged on either side of the river.

My Kayagar paddlers called out, "Hadi! Tuan Don is here!"

There was a rapid scurrying inside the longhouses as some of the occupants, awakened from their afternoon naps, prepared to flee, while one or two others took the time to see who was coming. These recognized me and came down excitedly from their homes to welcome us to their village. Hadi was working in the jungle, but messengers soon found him and brought him back. It was like a reunion of old friends.

Hadi invited me up into his home and we sat down to talk, using the still meager Sawi vocabulary I had learned from him. I still had no idea what grammatical rules might govern word order in this never-before-analyzed language, but still he seemed to understand most of what I said.

At this point I mentioned for the first time that I was on my way to Kamur's old village site to build my home. Hadi sat stunned in disbelief, wondering if perhaps he had misunderstood my mutilated Sawi. I repeated the statement emphatically, and it got through. Hadi translated it for the others gathering around and immediately a chorus of little whistles and exclamations signaled the excitement running through the village.

"I want you to come to Kamur and help me build my home, Hadi," I said.

"*Der!* Good!" he replied, breaking out in a wide smile, "I'll come tomorrow!"

As I rose to leave, Hadi laid a hand on my shoulder and pointed to the other end of the longhouse where a young man lay sick, too delirious to share in the excitement of the moment.

"My son Amwi is very sick," he said. "Can you help him?"

I made my way to the emaciated youth, ducking under overhead racks heavy with bows, arrows, spears and the sago-sifting tools used by the swamp-dwellers. Not yet experienced in reading the symptoms of tropical diseases, I took a guess that it was malaria, and administered the appropriate drug.

Hadi and I then embraced each other as a gesture of farewell, and I left Yohwi. Hadi followed us along the swampy edge of the Baitom, assuring me over and over that he would meet me at Kamur as soon as he could gather enough sago to last him for a few days. Then the jungle hid him from view.

At five o'clock that evening we reached the site of Kamur's old, rotting village, which was about to undergo a dramatic rejuvenation. There was still no sign of any Sawi at the location. Nor did we have time to go looking for them, with only an hour of daylight left. We chose one of the least dilapidated of the longhouses and hoisted our goods up into it. The floor was still strong enough to support our weight, with the exception of a few gaping holes. We cooked our evening meal and spread out our grass mats for the night.

Just before dawn next morning we awakened to hear a wall of rain advancing upon us. Within a few seconds it struck the old longhouse with such force the building seemed to sway. Not until mid-morning did the rain allow us to begin the day's work.

I appointed the six workers at my disposal as follows: two were to travel up the tributary to try to find Kamur, bearing gifts to the chiefs of the village and inviting them to come out and meet with me. Three others were to set out with axes and cut ironwood piers for the foundation of my home. The one remaining worker stayed to help me clear the land.

Soon the five were gone, leaving a young man named Hedip and myself to tackle the formidable tangle of vines that ensnarled the proposed location of our home. We plunged in, flailing with our machetes. The jungle began to yield ground, slowly and reluctantly, but it was all low ground! I knew if we built our home on land like that we would have water standing under our floor for months at a time during rainy seasons.

We slashed in deeper until Hedip pointed his machete in among the twisted roots at his feet. I looked, and sure enough, the land was sloping upward! We concentrated our energies to follow the slope and, to our intense delight, saw it rise to the unbelievable height of four feet above the surrounding swampland! A knoll of ground as high as that was a rarity in the area and would probably not yield to flooding more than a few weeks out of every year.

Stephen would have dry ground to play on after all!

About two hours later our clearing operation was interrupted by the return of the two gift-bearers I had sent to search for Kamur. They beamed happily and said, "We found them, Tuan."

I said, "Where are they?"

A Kayagar raised his paddle and pointed back upstream. I looked and saw five or six dugouts inching closer beyond a screen of foliage. I still could not see the men who stood in the dugouts, but I knew they were watching me.

The two Kayagar called to them, and presently one canoe and then another and another inched forward through the foliage screen, revealing two or three dozen taut-muscled, wary Sawi warriors. Their eyes were fixed upon me and they made no sound, as they gradually responded to the Kayagar's coaxing and came closer. Their palmwood bows lay strung and ready at their feet as they stood naked in their dugouts.

I stood near the water's edge and said, *"Kona-hario!"*

No answer. Their canoes nudged the shore and still they stood staring. Now that they were closer, I could detect the trembling of their limbs and the nervous twitching of their eyebrows. I was trembling a bit myself but managed to keep it inside where it couldn't be seen. This time there was no John or Ken to give advice, no *Ebenezer* or skiff for a hasty retreat if the situation took a bad turn.

A meeting of culturally similar strangers is one thing, but a meeting of culturally dissimilar strangers is something else! Representing opposite ends of humanity's wide-ranging cultural spectrum, we faced

130

each other, and the very air between us seemed to crackle with tension.

Hoary millenniums earlier, their ancestors and mine had been one people, living together, using the same tools and weapons, pursuing the same goals, speaking the same language. Then they had wandered apart, not merely into differing climes, but into steadily diverging life-styles as well. Genetic variations in metabolism, skin color, hair, and body proportions had emerged and become distilled through mutual isolation. Linguistic change had obliterated the original mother tongue, leaving orphaned the various offspring languages, which continued to diverge until they could no longer recognize each other as siblings.

And now, after aeons of change had metamorphosed us both until we appeared totally alien to each other, providence had brought us together again to demonstrate. . . .

While the younger men remained in their dugouts, three of the more mature strangers cautiously stepped ashore and approached me. The Kayagar, having failed in their attempt to prevent me from coming to the Sawi, now seemed to have changed their attitude completely. I could see they were taking great pleasure and pride in their role as the facilitators of this new encounter. Fussing like nursemaids, they coaxed the Sawi closer, gently chiding them for their almost rude reticence.

One of the three men suddenly stepped right up to me. His right eye had earlier been pierced by an arrow and had rotted out, but his left eye held me with a sagacious gleam. I raised my hand toward him. He responded.

For a brief moment we took one another's measure, and then we touched fingers. Gradually the emotional static diminished, the feeling of fiery strangeness subsided. We were equally human . . . flesh and blood . . . men.

He smiled at me and said, "I am Hato!"

Gripping his hand, I replied, "I am Don!"

The other two men crowded in and touched my hand also. They said in turn:

"I am Kigo!"

"I am Numu!"

The three heroes had emerged again!

Their companions then thronged up from the canoes, and the air rang with *Konaharios!* I pointed to the newly cleared ground and indicated my intent to build a house and live there. They responded, *"Der! Der! Der!* Good! Good! Good!" I asked them to bring split palm tree bark for the floor, and they promised to return with it the next day.

Suddenly their cries and exclamations grew louder, swelling in a unified wave of rejoicing which crested and broke in a mighty, deep-chested shout called *hahap kaman.* It was a shout in which no one expressed his joy fully until all expressed it together. It aroused in me such a feeling of mingled strangeness and hope that my scalp began to tingle. They made me feel as if someone had just hit a home run in a world series ball game. And as every eye was fixed

upon me, I gathered that I was the one! I could hardly keep my feet on the ground!

As the great shout began to subside, another sound welled up beneath it. I swung around to see the Kronkel black with the canoes of Amyam and Yohwi. Hadi and all his band were skimming toward us, rumbling their paddle blades loudly on the sides of their dugouts. The sight and the sound of them immediately triggered another ecstatic response in the men of Kamur. Before Kamur's second *hahap kaman* died down, Yohwi and Amyam suddenly ceased their rapping and thundered forth their own *hahap kaman*, waving their paddles and springing in their canoes to make waves.

The vocal cannonades resounded again and again, hurling volley after volley back and forth between the shore and the river. It was the Sawi equivalent of a twenty-one gun salute. And it signaled the end of an aeon of isolation, the dawn of an era of interaction.

If I had not been there that day to trigger that salute as an emissary of Christ, someone else's emissary would have triggered it later, possibly with quite different motives and results. Those who advocate that the world's remaining tribal groups should be left to themselves do not realize how naive their notion is! The world just isn't big enough anymore for *anyone* to be left alone! It is a foregone conclusion that even if missionaries do not go in to *give*, lumbermen, crocodile hunters, prospectors, or farmers will still go in to *take!* The issue is not then, should anyone go in, because obviously *someone* will! The issue is rather, will the most sympathetic person get there first?

As the one who got there first to live among the Sawi, it was my aim to combine faithfulness to God and the Scriptures with respect for the Sawi and their culture. The crucial question was, would Sawi culture and the Scriptures prove so opposite in their basic premises as to render this two-way loyalty impossible? I intended to find out.

But first I had to build my home.

9

Gods from the Sky

With more workers available we soon completed the clearing of the land. By that time the Kayagar had returned with a canoeload of ironwood piers and stringers, so I lined up the location of the house in the center of the knoll of high ground and began setting piers in place. I am not a trained carpenter, but working with John McCain on the construction of a small storehouse at Pirimapun had taught me some of the basic principles of building with cut poles which is quite different from building with sawn timber.

Before long the canoes of Haenam also arrived. Word of my coming had reached them at their retreat deep in the jungles south of the Kronkel. I now became a lone, white speck in the midst of a milling crowd of about two hundred Kayagar, Atohwaem and Sawi, three tribes which had often regarded each other as enemies and seldom as friends. Every man among them was capable of flying into a rage at the mere drop of a word. Most of them carried their spear-paddles or had bone daggers stuck in their armbands. Their bows also were strung and ready in their canoes. It was difficult to concentrate on building, as I kept looking over my shoulder to try to detect any brewing of trouble before it broke out. Still I managed to square the house reasonably well.

As the hours passed, I was amazed at the deep-seated composure God was breathing into me. I seemed to be sealed inside a capsule of peace, which cushioned every alarming development and added a note of authority to my voice, making the few words I knew go a long way. These wild men of the swamps responded to my requests as if they had no choice but to obey them.

Once the sixteen piers were all in place at five-foot intervals, I set up a pile-driving operation to drive them deeper into the clay. I called upon various groups of men to take turns climbing up on a make-shift platform to raise the pile driver and let it fall. This proved to be a splendid diversionary tactic; their attention was transfixed by it. Laughter and excitement filled the air.

But once the pile driving was over, the murmurings started again, and hard looks began to dart back and forth. Just then a tall Kayagar chief named Yae broke forth in a rumbling torrent of words. I was hard pressed to tell whether he was exhorting the assembly to keep the peace or simply venting feelings of resentment against the Sawi. Fearful that it might be the latter, I stepped up behind him and laid a gentle hand on his shoulder. Since I knew no Kayagar words profound enough for the occasion, I simply talked to him soothingly in English. Yae immediately quieted down, as did others who were beginning to get excited.

But before long mutterings of tension began to seethe again. I was concerned lest the day of my arrival should forever become associated in the minds of the Sawi with memories of bloodshed. And feeling that there was nothing more I could do to forestall an impending conflict, I laid down my tools and simply asked God to intervene. At that moment the hum of an aircraft engine sounded from the heavens, quelling instantly the tumult of disquieted warriors.

Of course! In the excitement of the afternoon I had completely forgotten that John McCain had arranged by radio for the Missionary Aviation Fellowship pilots to attempt a first float-plane landing on the Kronkel that very day and bring me a load of kerosene. Earlier in the day I had tried to forewarn the assembly of warriors that the aircraft would soon arrive, but as far as I could tell, they had not understood what I was saying.

Thanking God for His perfect timing, I took off my shirt ready to wave a signal to the pilots when they flew overhead, and then settled back to observe the reactions of my tempestuous companions. All of these tribesmen had, of course, seen or heard aircraft passing over at great heights. Many of them also had memories of aircraft making low passes over some of their villages years earlier, probably Australian military aircraft searching for signs of Japanese incursion, or vice versa. They were convinced that all aircraft were supernatural beings in their own right, and had not yet learned to associate them with Tuans.

Their standard reaction to the approach of an aircraft was to flee into dense underbrush and cower in terror. In fact, years earlier, some dreamer had successfully propagated the notion that *aramaso*, "aircraft," were allergic to thorns, hence the safest place to hide was among thorns. This notion was perfectly true, of course, since no airplane does want thorns in its tires. But it also caused the people much suffering, for after an aircraft had passed by, they would first pick themselves up out of the thorns and then spend several days picking the thorns out of themselves. It had, however, been many years since an aircraft had made a low pass, and never in the history of the area had one been known to actually land!

Wild-eyed, the warriors scanned the white-and-blue checkerboard of cloud and sky for some sign of the droning intruder, hoping against hope that it would pass by in the distance. Suddenly there it was, low and black against the clouds, whirring along over a distant bend of the Kronkel, and then abruptly turning to follow another bend straight toward us! Quavering cries broke out all around me, swelling together into a uniformly high-pitched scream of sheer panic. Men and boys stampeded in waves toward the jungle. How glad I was that there were no women and children present to suffer this severe fright.

As the aircraft zoomed over on its first pass I waved my shirt and saw the wing dip in acknowledgement. Then I walked down to the riverbank to await the landing and found to my surprise a small group of men huddled together, trembling in fear, yet refusing to flee.

Kigo and Hato were among them, but Numu apparently had decided that this was too much! The others were a number of chiefs who seemingly had understood my earlier attempt to explain the coming of the aircraft and so assumed that the *aramaso* meant them no harm, but was simply coming to meet the Tuan.

They wanted to see what sort of wondrous transactions took place when the god from the sky met the god on the ground!

Crew-cut Hank Worthington eyed the long black ribbon of the *kidari*, searching for deadheads or other obstructions that might disqualify it as a float landing site. Satisfied that it was clear, he next buzzed the surface and then roared out again over the treetops to try to ascertain the clearance for takeoff. Beside him sat blond Paul Pontier, also a veteran of many hazardous first landings in remote areas of Netherlands New Guinea.

The two pilots glanced at each other and nodded in agreement. Hank swung the Cessna 180 around again and shoe-horned it down between towering walls of jungle. The soaring ironwood trees and ramshackle longhouses on the far bend loomed rapidly closer, as if seen through a zooming telescopic lens.

I glanced at Hato. His whole body was streaming with sweat as with his one good eye he followed the downward swoop of "Mike Papa Bravo." Kigo and the others shuddered and began to back away as twin plumes of white spray poofed under the floats. At that point Hank Worthington gunned the engine in order to keep the aircraft up "on the step" for an easy approach to the shore. Hato's muscles melted into water and he cowered behind me for refuge.

For a brief moment I seemed to absorb the feelings of the frightened men around me! I found myself looking at the float plane from the viewpoint of the stone age, and I shuddered! Then the feeling passed and I became once more a twentieth century man waiting for a float plane to bring a load of kerosene.

As Hank cut the engine, the shouting of the multitude took over in full force. Looking back over my shoulder, I saw dozens of men half-hidden at the edge of the forest. Many held their arms outstretched toward the Cessna, writhing their fingers as if to keep it at bay.

Suddenly Hank and Paul swung open the doors on either side of the Cessna, triggering another explosion of alarmed cries. Then they climbed down onto the floats and gasps of amazement went up on all sides. In that moment a great mystery was cleared up—the *aramaso* were only vehicles of the Tuans! Still, the friendly, English-speaking voices which greeted me from the floats seemed to them to come from another world.

The floats struck ground about ten feet out from shore, so I waded out and brought Hank ashore on my back, while Paul Pontier unloaded jerry cans of kerosene. At first none of the Sawi would come near to help us, but gradually I coaxed Hato and Kigo to come closer. They touched hands with Hank and saw he was an approachable being.

After that they were willing to wade out under the shadow of those great stretching yellow-and-black wings and bring the jerry cans ashore. We opened one of the two 55-gallon drums I had brought from Kawem and funneled about ten jerry cans of kerosene into it. While the kerosene was flowing Hank gazed at the leaping, shouting swarm of slightly reassured warriors emerging from the bush.

Then he looked at me inquisitively and asked, "Is everything all right?"

"Just fine," I replied. I didn't tell him his arrival had possibly just averted an outbreak of fighting between mutually antagonistic groups among the people.

"We've just come from Kawem. Your wife and son are well. She sent you a letter," Hank explained, handing me an envelope with Carol's handwriting on it.

Paul joined in, "And here's a package she sent you!" He tossed it from the plane and I caught it.

When they were ready to leave, Paul Pontier leaned on a wing strut and shook his head. The sun was getting low, and wild-eyed, stringy-haired men with curved pig tusks jutting from their nostrils were crowding closer again.

"Just from the natural look of things, I'd say, 'Get in this plane and let us whisk you out of here!'" Paul said. "But I guess you wouldn't want to leave, would you?" He was testing me, in case under the surface I had lost my nerve and needed rescuing.

"Nothing doing, Paul," I replied. "I'm just getting started."

"Okay," he said. "You take care now and we'll be praying."

Paul climbed up into the cabin as Hank waved good-bye and slammed his door shut. One tip of the Cessna's wing was within reach, so I laid hold of it and swung the airplane around to face the open channel of the Kronkel.

The prop flicked once and then the engine roared to life. Spray whipped up from the Kronkel struck us like driving rain, scattering tribesmen like leaves in the wind. Standing alone by the river, I watched "Mike Papa Bravo" race furiously down the *kidari*, lift above the trees and vanish among the clouds.

It was now late afternoon and most of the tribesmen present dispersed in their canoes to reach their respective villages before dark. As they left, I gave them instructions on the type of jungle building materials they should return with on the morrow, if they intended to return. A few others resorted to the dilapidated longhouses for shelter, so as to be on hand for work first thing in the morning.

The last problem I faced that day was how to take a bath! I was too wary of crocodiles, poisonous snakes and leeches to risk a plunge into the Kronkel, so I simply stood by the river in my shorts and scooped up buckets of water, poured them over me, soaped myself and then used more bucketfuls to wash the soap off.

Of course everyone around left his cooking fire untended to come and observe this unique operation. It was the first time they had ever seen soap or its use. I could feel their eyes devouring my white skin, and wondered at the excited murmur of conversation buzzing around me.

Later I learned that it was not only my white skin they were commenting on—they were also concerned as they watched the soap suds flowing from my skin down into the Kronkel. For they knew that with those soap suds a new foreign element of great potential consequence was being introduced into their river— my skin-grease!

"What will the spirits think?" they were asking. "How will they react?"

For better or for worse, I had indeed placed my skin-grease in the Kronkel River, not knowing that in the eyes of the people, this was equivalent to throwing a gauntlet in front of the demons who claimed control of the Sawi universe!

The challenge had been given. The struggle could begin at any time.

I saw myself standing among flaring buttresses of

gigantic ironwood trees, feeling very small, oppressed with dread and sinking to my ankles in the soft jungle floor.

I was not alone. From among the buttresses a host of Sawi men slowly emerged. First among them was Hato. He came and stood before me, his one eye probing my being with unspeakable solemnity. His lips moved in speech, but I could hear no voice. He seemed to charge me with some intensely urgent responsibility.

Then Kigo stood beside Hato, speaking more words I could not hear, his black eyes pleading inexorably. Husky Tumo, Numu's son, was next to fix me with his gaze, followed by Hadi, Er, and others whose names and faces I was just beginning to know. Some of them pointed to themselves and then gestured toward their women and children, who were watching concernedly from the borders of the swampscape surrounding us.

I found myself becoming totally sensitized to the intrinsic humanity of each individual. Uncouth, mis-shapen, scarred, facially peculiar, or covered with flaking fungus infections as some of them were, they were all intensely appealing in their mute acknowl-edgement of some deep, inexpressible need.

Their urgency was like that of doomed men seeking reprieve. And they were charging me with respon-sibility for that reprieve. The pressure of that respon-sibility became an intolerable burden.

Suddenly I awoke, sweating, heaving with desire to bring solace to those grimly anxious men and to their women and children. For about an hour I lay desolate with longing before God, pleading with Him that the reprieve written in blood so long ago might soon be made effective for these lost sheep of the swamps. Just before sunrise He breathed in the assurance I was seeking.

The dawn first whispered the secret of its coming to the *Haragu* birds, who bugled it to the birds-of-paradise, who fluted it to the cockatoos, who blared it to the loris, who fifed it to all the twittering, trumpeting, warbling denizens in the teeming attics of the forest. Together they brought forth a swelling opus of sound as opulent as the dawn-glow itself.

We started work early, wrestling heavy ironwood stringers into position atop the piers and then spiking them in place. Later John McCain arrived with the *Ebenezer* and a load of mangrove poles for the floor joists. Together we laid the floor with split palm bark and framed the walls and the roof with cut poles. Then we worked on porches, doors, windows, stairs and kitchen counters while Sawi and Kayagar workers thatched the roof and filled in the walls with sago fronds.

On July 10 we paid the workers, and I set out for Kawem, leaving the Sawi with one brief message: "In three days' time I'll return . . . with my wife and child."

10

Destiny in a Dugout

Broad-shouldered, lean-hipped, the six Kayagar men dipped their spear-paddles in rhythmic unison, impelling our narrow craft across mile after sweltering mile of flooded grassland. Ahead, a troupe of spindly egrets studied our approach from the branches of a lone island of *ahos* trees. As the sharp prow of our dugout sliced rapidly closer, they suddenly took flight, wafting weightlessly to the next island of *ahos* trees, where they settled until we overtook them again. In this manner, like albatross accompanying a ship at sea, they led our dugout across the sun-drenched ocean of grass.

From under the shade canopy I had rigged in the center of the canoe, two intensely communicative blue eyes peeked over Carol's shoulder. Seeing me, they first softened in intimate recognition, and then popped wide with wonder at the white flash of an egret skimming by. A tiny hand reached out to touch the swishing *kunai* grass. A clear voice, tinkling with baby delight, exclaimed over the headlong flight of a flock of whistling ducks. A puckish face looked up in awe at the rasping passage of a pair of grotesque hornbills.

With the keen awareness of a seven-month-old child, Stephen was beginning to respond to his new environment. He found it utterly delightful. He could sense no danger in it. He reveled in its beauty until, fulfilled by myriad new sensations of light and sound and texture, he settled back to nurse and then to sleep, lulled by the gentle rocking of the canoe.

Far ahead a horizon lined with dark green jungle shimmered in the heat of noon. Gradually it loomed nearer, and then suddenly we left the grasslands behind, gliding under the shade of overhanging trees into the main course of the Kronkel. Borne along by the westward flow of the river, we soon passed Amyam, where men, women and children stared incredulously at their first vision of a golden-haired woman and the equally golden-haired child reclining in her lap.

The sun was now well past the zenith. Our paddlers grew weary as the breezeless torpor of late afternoon lay heavy on the swamp. Carol wet her handkerchief in the river to cool Stephen's forehead. The intense heat and humidity cast their spell over our perceptions—time appeared to slow down until even the fish were jumping in slow motion, and the long bends of the Kronkel stretched ever longer as we traversed them.

I was concerned that we reach our destination before dark.

Standing in his canoe, Narai thrust the point of his paddle deep into a clump of elephant grass. Next he placed the blade of the paddle across the walls of his canoe and sat on it. Thus anchored by the elephant grass, he waited, gazing steadily upstream.

Narai's pulse quickened as he reflected on the strange events of past months, events unprecedented in Sawi history. The terrifying intrusion of the two riverboats . . . the sudden encounter with three Tuans on the *kidari* . . . the spellbinding odyssey of Hadi and Er . . . the first Sawi journey to Pirimapun . . . the return of one of the Tuans to build a home beside the Tumdu . . . the landing of the *aramaso* . . . the coming of the Kawem Tuan a few days later to help finish the house, and finally . . . the departure of both Tuans, one of them promising to return three days later with his wife and child.

Or had they misunderstood his sign language?

It was now the third day. Three miles downstream, the combined populations of Haenam, Kamur and Yohwi were massed and ready. Spaced at intervals along the intervening bends of the river, other watchers were waiting to relay whatever signal Narai might give.

Time and the Kronkel drifted by.

Narai glanced over his shoulder at the lowering

sun. Perhaps the Tuan who for incomprehensible reasons had appeared out of nowhere to build beside the Tumdu had decided that. . . .

Far upstream, a flash of sun on wet paddles caught Narai's attention. The sleek black line of a Kayagar dugout swept into view, dipping through shimmering reflections toward the lone watcher. Narai crouched forward in his canoe, slowly disengaging his paddle from the elephant grass.

But still he waited. Then he saw an auspicious gleam of color among the Kayagar paddlers. Standing tall in his dugout, he raised a bamboo horn to his lips and blew a long, low-pitched blast.

Within a few seconds the signal was relayed to the distant village. Smiling expectantly, Narai prepared to escort the approaching craft to its destination. The sun was already only a mass of incandescent points sinking beyond a bamboo screen.

Suddenly a lone Sawi was there, paddling beside us.

"Konahari!" I called.

"Konahari!" he replied, smiling.

Soon a second and later a third escort materialized out of the blue haze of evening, skimming over the Kronkel in miniature dugouts hardly more than twelve feet long. By the time we rounded the last bend, six or seven of the small craft were added to our convoy, their occupants calling ahead in their mysterious, flowing language, and ending each sentence with a long emphatic ". . . oooooo!"

150

Down the last stretch, Carol and I peered ahead through legs and paddles, trying to catch a first glimpse of our home and of. . . ? We were not prepared for what we saw! About two hundred armed warriors thronged the shore, looming into stark silhouette against a red-gold horizon. Feathers bristled from their hair and fluttered from their spears. Further back, and closer to the small cut-pole house John and I had completed three days earlier, an equal number of women and small children watched us, exclaiming in hushed tones over our strange appearance.

Our paddlers grew silent as we glided in and struck shore at the feet of the armed multitude.

11

A Baptism of Strangeness

"Look at them!" Carol breathed.

Closer now, we could see garish white and ocher paint smeared on their faces in such a way as to make their eye sockets, by contrast, look like gaping black holes. We could see in detail the spiny ridges of barbs tapering up to the points of their spears. We could hear the thin sizzle of their whispering, rising in pitch as excitement welled up within them.

It was hard to believe they were the same people who only days before had so meekly gathered materials for our home. Then it had been easy to forget that behind their friendly mannerisms and disarming enthusiasm, they were *still* headhunters and cannibals. Now they really looked the part.

Had I misread their intentions? Was this their way of expressing welcome, or was it something else? Had

I missed God's leading in bringing Carol and Stephen here so soon? I could hear my heart pounding as if in an echo chamber.

Some of the Sawi stepped into the water and gripped the sides of our dugout.

"Lord God, have I been a fool? These men have never even learned to respect a policeman, let alone honor You—and here we are: man, wife and child, sixty-five river-miles from the nearest government post—defenseless except for Your Spirit surrounding us.

"Is it only human presumption, instead of Your peace, that has been sustaining us?"

As the Sawi drew our dugout higher onto the mud bank, the answer came from within my own heart. That peace, if it was only human presumption, still had one essential thing in its favor—in the moment of crisis *it was still there!* Surely, I thought, if it was not from God, it would have deserted me now! Unimpressed by the alarm of my senses, amused by the warnings of mere reason, that peace kept reinforcing my inmost core.

But what about Carol? And Stephen?

Kneeling, I reached under the canopy and lifted Stephen from Carol's lap. From my arms, he beamed a cherubic smile at the war-painted host, reaching toward them with his own chubby arms. Carol slipped out from under the canopy and stood beside me. She was awed, excited, but revealed no trace of anxiety.

Warily, the Kayagar paddlers in the front part of the dugout stepped ashore, clearing our way. We proceeded to the tip of the canoe and stepped off into the midst of the crowd. The other three paddlers followed, shouldering our equipment.

Someone seized my right arm. Hadi! He was intoxicated with excitement. Another hand gripped my shoulder. Hato! His one eye gleamed with a light of its own. Older Sawi women were fondling Carol and Stephen incredulously. Men were crowding closer as dusk fell.

I handed Stephen to Carol that my arms might be free to clear a way through the crowd toward our home, still fifty yards distant. The warriors, however, were now packed so tightly around us it was impossible to move. We could do nothing but submit to their will and stand waiting.

Suddenly the suppressed whispering around us began to swell into a cry of *esa! esa! esa!* From somewhere behind me, a lone voice shrieked a high-pitched command. A signal. For what?

Carol's gaze met mine, while Stephen quickly searched both our faces. Her clear, blue eyes were still radiant, trustful, without the slightest suggestion of, "Why have you brought us here?" Seeing her look, Stephen relaxed again on her shoulder, and I knew as never before I had chosen the right woman.

The test was not yet over, however.

Triggered by the loud signal, a heavy fusillade of drum-beating exploded around us, making us shudder involuntarily. Peering through the crowd, I saw one of the drums. Thin-waisted, flared at both ends, both its body and its full-length handle was engraved with exotic ancestral designs. The drumhead itself was of speckled black lizard-skin glued on with human blood, dark rivulets of which had been allowed to trickle down the sides of the drum, drying to form part of its decor.

The otherness of the Sawi.

Gradually the drummers synchronized their rhythms into a steady, booming thunder, whereupon the entire host erupted in a paroxysm of wild shouting, leaping in the air, jabbing their spears up and down. Standing at the heart of the tumult, we studied the wildly animated faces of the celebrants, awed by the fierce intensity of their emotion, their absolute involvement in the meaning of the moment.

Presently the shouting became chanting, the leaping gave way to dancing. Wave after wave of warriors swirled closer, as if to engulf us. It's like a baptism, I thought. A baptism of primitive spirit. Of strangeness.

Suddenly, in the blue glow of twilight, a Presence stronger than the presence of the multitude enveloped us. The same Presence that had first drawn us to trust in Christ, and then wooed us across continents and oceans to this very jungle clearing. Before that Presence, every superficial thought and feeling fled away, and I felt a deep probe go through my motives.

"Missionary," He was asking, "why are you here?"

It was a question I had often fielded from the lips of unbelievers. Now my Lord was asking it, and there was no escape from the question. The eyes of every Sawi dancer seemed to ask it. Their voices seemed to chant it, their drums to echo it.

I reviewed answers I had used in the past, discarding them one by one. Secondary, incidental reasons

157

no longer mattered. Nor could ulterior ambitions endure the four-dimensional reality our task had now assumed.

The descent to new bedrock took a few minutes. Then I breathed my answer:

"Lord Jesus, it is for You we stand here, immersed not in water but in Sawi humanity. This is our baptism into the work You anticipated for us before creation. Keep us faithful. Empower us with Your Spirit.

"May Your will be done among these people as it is in heaven. And if any good comes to them through us, the honor is Yours!"

And He replied, "The peace of God, which passes all understanding, shall garrison your hearts and minds through Christ."

It was all right now. Our relationship was renewed. I could feel a fresh spring welling up inside.

Suddenly the multitude was moving through the deep shadows, bearing us toward our home. They parted to allow us access to the rough steps I had fashioned earlier. We climbed together up onto the crude front porch and turned toward them. A tremendous shout made the air quiver. Men and boys were leaping up and down, drumming and chanting with great force. Beyond them, the women were dancing separately, their long grass skirts tossing like waves of the sea.

It was clear now, as we looked down into the upturned faces of the warriors, that they had not intended to frighten us. They carried their spears in

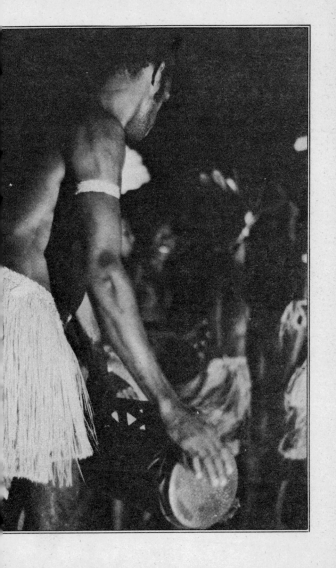

the same way a military honor guard carries bayonets.
Every motion, every dab of paint and every cadence
of sound was for our pleasure.

The Kayagar somehow made their way through
the crowd with our supplies. I took a flashlight from
one pack and led the way into the house, Carol
following with wide-eyed Stephen. Seeing us enter,
the Sawi began to dance slowly around our dwelling
until they surrounded it on all sides. The tumult of
voices, drums and stamping feet seemed about to
break in through the thin, sago-frond walls of the
small home.

Together we surveyed the interior of our new resi-
dence by flashlight. Around our feet scores of black
crickets scurried to hide from the beam, while overhead a large, green tree-frog with bulging eyes leaped
frantically from rafter to rafter. But the frog's were
not the only black eyes watching us. Turning, I saw
that a number of dancers had left the singing and
crowded onto our porch to stare at us through the
window screen.

Under their close scrutiny, I pumped up a kerosene
pressure lamp and turned it on, forgetting that this
was the first time I had used such a device among
the Sawi. There was a mad scramble as the unexpected burst of light struck their eyes. No one took
the time to find the stairs—they simply abandoned
ship by leaping over the railings. Fortunately the level
of our porch was only five feet above ground.

Outside, the drumming came to a sudden halt, and
the chanting boiled over into a wail. There was an
unmistakable sound of hundreds of feet stampeding

into the night. Setting the lamp on a counter, I hurried outside to reassure the people.

Then I saw why they had fled. Our entire home was agleam with light like some gigantic, awesome jack-o-lantern. Through hundreds of cracks in sago-frond walls, through every door and window, the blinding light of the little five-hundred-candlepower silk mantle was stabbing into the darkness.

We were not the only ones being baptized with strangeness.

"Tadan nomo! Tadan nomo! Kee nawain!" I called. "Don't be afraid! Come back!"

Slowly, Hadi, Hato and others returned, reassured to see that the intense light was only from an instrument and did not mean that Carol, Stephen and I had suddenly transformed ourselves into gods radiating awesome supernatural power.

Minutes later the drums began to throb again, as the dancers regained their composure and returned to encircle our house—though at a slightly wider radius.

While Carol cooked a simple meal on a primus, I spread our bedroll in a corner and hung a mosquito net over it. As soon as possible, all three of us were under the net. In spite of the thunder of drums just outside our wall, Stephen fell asleep in a few minutes, breathing softly beside us. Carol and I took a little longer.

Some of the dancers were now bearing torches, which glowed eerily through our sago-frond walls. "Close your eyes, honey," I whispered, "and tell me what you see."

She said, "I see miles of grassland slipping by, and egrets flying around us. I feel the canoe rocking. Now I see the sunset, and all those people dancing around us. But I'm not afraid. I feel so different, as if God has given me new emotional responses to enable me to live here."

He had indeed, and to me also.

That tight enclosure of human bodies—a throbbing womb of alien sound and psyche—had been a mold of God to transform us into creatures who could breathe, without toxic effect, the atmosphere of this primeval world, so that we might serve Him in this world also.

Provided, of course, we could first master its language and penetrate its mysteries.

12

Patriarch of the Tumdu

Hulking darkly through the shadows, the wild boar caught a scent of fresh sago pulp and veered toward it. Wedging his long snout under barriers of vegetation, he pressed on easily, letting tangles of vines and branches slide up the inclined plane of his bristling neck and down the steep slope of his back. He broke through into a small clearing awash with moonlight. Across the far side of the clearing lay a felled sago palm, its trunk gashed open on the side facing him. He lumbered toward it.

At the center of the clearing he halted abruptly, bracing all four hooves in the oozing jungle floor, ready for instant flight in any direction. A new scent was mixed with the sour tang of sago pulp—human scent.

With a brisk snort the boar swung his massive head from side to side, scanning warily. There was no movement except the shadow-drift of giant bats across the stars, no sound except the ringing of cicadas and the jangling of frog choirs in a nearby swamp.

The boar was no stranger to human scent. He had often encountered it, especially in clearings like this where humans had been working sago. But humans worked by day. The night belonged to him.

Emboldened, he sniffed closer to the aromatic gash in the sago trunk. He found that the pulp just inside the gash had already been hollowed out. To reach more he would have to thrust his head inside.

He scanned the underbrush one last time, moonlight gleaming on his curved tusks. Then he thrust his head inside the sago trunk and began to feed on the rich, flour-laden pulp. The hole was just the right size.

Immediately a long bamboo arrow slid forward through a gap in a nearby blind of sago fronds. From beyond the blind came a faint *tik* of a vine bowstring being stretched almost to the breaking point. The pig did not detect it. His ears were full of the sound of his own munching. But suddenly he felt himself spitted by a straight line of pain that led right through his heart. The arrow had gone clear through him.

Even before the hard vine bowstring stopped rattling, the pig had lurched free of the sago trunk, thunderous blasts of air exploding from his lungs. Squealing, he bolted toward the far side of the clearing, blood pouring from his body as if from two taps.

Suddenly he whirled to face whatever was tormenting him, but still no adversary was in sight. Then, his forelegs folded under him. Coughing blood, he rolled on his side and lay still.

Minutes later, the hunter emerged from behind the frond-screen, a second arrow fitted to his bow. He took his time approaching the pig and touched it with his foot, relaxing his bowstring when he saw the pig was dead.

Hato stalked back to the pig blind, and then returned bringing from it six of the shorter fronds. Spreading the fronds in three overlapping pairs around his prey, he knelt on the ground and began to weave together the overlapping leaves of each pair. The weaving completed, he took a narrow bamboo razor from a satchel, crouched over the dead pig and commenced the long task of butchering.

As he worked, an eerie nimbus of soft light encircled his naked body—the play of moonlight on the wings of hundreds of mosquitoes whirring about him. Overhead, fireflies shimmered among towering liana trellises, while in black recesses of the jungle, patches of phosphorescence gleamed from rotting vegetation like a host of luminous eyes.

Hato by moonlight.

That the universe might somewhere offer man anything other than a swamp environment had never occurred to him. And even if it had occurred to him, he could not have conceived of an environment more suitable for human habitation than this one which now bathed his senses.

Dividing the carcass into three heaps of pork, intestine and bone, he placed one part in the center of each of the pairs of interwoven sago fronds he had prepared. Then he folded the yet unwoven leaves over the meat and wove them together also, forming three strong packs, each containing about sixty pounds of pork and bone. Lastly, he tied shoulder straps of vine to each end of the various frond stems in each pack and then hoisted one onto his own back.

By this time dawn was breaking. Bending under the weight of the pack, Hato gathered together his bow and arrows, including the bloody one that had gone through the pig. Standing in the dim light of early dawn, he could have been mistaken for any one of his ancestors in every respect. Except one.

Returning to the pig blind, Hato reached down and picked up the new steel machete he had earned by helping the Tuan build his home, and which he had used to cut the fronds for his pig blind. The only difference, but it was a big one.

As the jungle awoke to the orchestrations of myriad forms of bird life, Hato headed for his treehouse dwelling near the source of the Tumdu. Two of his many sons would retrieve the other packs later.

Sirowi and Imati, two of Hato's four wives, took their places on opposite sides of a tall sago palm. Stolidly, they battered both sides of the palm with stone axes until the fibers in its heavy black casing grew weak. The giant tottered and crashed, burying one-third of its bulk in the soft jungle floor.

While Imati pried open the casing on one side, Sirowi set up the sago processing trough. Once the heart of the palm was exposed, both women commenced cutting out the fibrous, flour-bearing pulp with stone adzes. Next they would wash the fibers in the trough, draining off the life-sustaining sago flour in solution.

To one side Imati's two-week-old baby lay blinking at the brightening sky, cushioned on a soft bed of leaves. Yami, one of Hato's granddaughters, waved a leaf over the baby to keep the jungle's omnipresent flies away from its face.

High overhead, a young boy named Badep clung to the topmost branches of a *kabi* tree, keeping watch lest Asmat raiders seeking human heads should be drawn toward the women by the sound of their chopping. He especially kept an eye on flocks of cockatoos circling here and there above the forest. Any unusual disturbance among them might indicate the approach of an enemy. It was not without basis that the Sawi often called the cockatoo *ragedep,* "the revealer."

Another of Hato's offspring, a lithe-limbed teen-age boy named Amio, slipped noiselessly through the swamp glades which were the main source of the Tumdu tributary. Above him eighty-foot-tall sago palms towered toward the sun, their great fronds arching together to form a many-vaulted ceiling over shadowy pools below. Weightlessly, Amio skirted the main pools, leaping from one grotesque root formation to another.

Suddenly in one pool the leap of a catfish arrested his attention. Amio squatted on a root and waited, bow and arrow in hand. A second fish jumped and then a third. Amio stood up and scanned the trees around him.

Finally, among the pillar-like palms he located an *os* tree. Drawing a new steel knife from his woven grass belt, the only item of clothing he wore, Amio stripped several slabs of bark from the side of the chosen tree. The inner side of each slab gleamed with thick, white sap. Amio carried the slabs to the side of the pool, held them under the surface of the water and began rubbing them together.

Soon a white cloudiness spread out toward the center of the pool, and down into its tea-dark depths. Amio repeated this operation on various sides of the pool until all of the white sap was dissolved in the water. Then he cast the bark aside, picked up his bow again and fitted a fish-arrow to the vine. He did not have to wait long.

Soon a fish broke the surface, gaping with pain, its eyes clouded over with the whitish substance. Amio's first arrow pierced its body; the fish thrashed about, still at the surface, dragging the arrow with it. When it passed close enough, Amio caught the end of the arrow and lifted his prey out of the water.

By this time several more blinded fish were cleaving the surface. He caught them all. Then he too made a pack out of sago fronds and wrapped the fish up inside it. But not until he had first removed the poisonous spines from the dorsal fins of the catfish. It would not do to hoist the pack onto one's back only to feel such a spine jabbing into one's flesh through the leaves.

Amio headed for the treehouse. He reached it about the time his two older brothers, Hanay and Wagay, returned with the two packs of fresh pork their father, Hato, had left in the jungle. Two other of Hato's wives, meanwhile, were cooking the pork Hato himself had earlier carried back from his night's hunting.

Kimi and Sayo, two of Hato's older daughters, conversed softly as they made their way through a thicket of young sago palms, their long grass skirts swaying as they gracefully avoided the masses of six-inch thorns which guard the bases of such palms in their earlier stages. Stooping by the edge of one of the Tumdu's limpid pools, they reached down into the water and lifted out two sacks made of woven fronds, which they had deposited two days earlier.

Each of the two sacks was filled with a mass of soft, cottony fibers consisting of embryonic leaves the girls had taken from inside the tip of a felled sago palm. As the water slowly drained out of the two sacks, the girls noted with delight the wriggling movements of a number of freshwater shrimp that had taken shelter in the two masses of fiber. Shrimp never could resist such ideal hiding places.

Kimi and Sayo deftly broke off several six-foot-long blades of elephant grass, wrapped up the live crustaceans, and then lowered the two shrimp traps again into the murky shallows of the Tumdu. They proceeded from pool to pool in this way until they completed a circuit to the point where they had left their carrying bags and digging sticks. Depositing the bundles of shrimp inside the voluminous sacks, they next took their sharpened palmwood digging sticks and cut a path into a lush forest of elephant grass, breaking off the thick stems just below water level. Stripping the massive leaves, they bared the edible core of each plant, heaping these inside their packs.

Shouldering their packs, they headed toward the treehouse, stopping here and there to pluck edible new leaves from the branches of a *sinaham* tree, or to shake ripe fruit from an *akakor*. Occasionally they would stoop to pluck a blood-sucking leech from their feet or ankles, tossing it aside without even a break in the flow of their conversation.

Meanwhile Sirowi and Imati had washed about seventy pounds of sago flour through the trough. Once this had settled out of solution, they drained off the water and burned the outside of each sago lump with flaming torches to make the gooey exterior congeal. The congealed exteriors were then peeled off and divided among all present for a wholesome midday snack.

A number of children had come from the treehouse for this special treat. Their laughter rippled as they stretched the rubbery *du rayp*, "sago mucous," until it broke and snapped back into their hands. While the children chewed the sago, Sirowi and Imati wrapped the moist loaves into packs to carry home.

As the various food-gatherers reached the base

of the treehouse, they first deposited their bundles of provisions in the family's three dugouts beached among the reeds by the Tumdu and then climbed up into their lofty home. Hato had given word that today they would all return to the village, so there was no point in lifting the heavy loads up into the treehouse.

The provisions were bountiful indeed. Besides pork, sago, fish, shrimp, elephant grass cores, edible leaves and fruit, there were also bundles of squirming beetle grubs, a death adder Hanay had killed with an arrow while returning with the pork, and a bird which Badep had shot while keeping watch for Asmat raiders. Some of the younger boys had also bagged a number of frogs and a lizard.

Assembled on a level with the treetops, the members of the family chewed on cuts of roasted pork while they listened to Hato's account of the killing of the boar. Now refreshed after a morning's rest, the one-eyed elder held one of the boar's ears in his hands as he talked. A woodtick looking for a new home crawled from the ear onto his hand. Hato casually flicked it into the fire smoking beside him.

Using a bamboo razor, he carved a circular piece of hairy flesh out of the middle of the boar's ear, and then cut a hole in the center of the piece of flesh, making it into a ring. Fitting this ring on the end of his bow, he worked it down to join similar trophies of pigs he had killed earlier.

All the while a blood-stained, four-foot-long, cane-shafted arrow lay beside him on the grass mat.

It was only an occasional arrow that found its way through the entire breadth of a pig's body without striking bone. And even then, only a rare bowman could shoot an arrow with sufficient force to drive it all the way through.

Hato was that kind of bowman, with four wives who lived at peace with him, the reverence of eleven living sons and daughters, the delights of a growing covey of grandchildren, and the dread of his enemies on all sides. Hato, the patriarch who lived at the source of the Tumdu.

What more did he need? He looked down at the new machete. He ran a finger along its gleaming edge. What more *did* he need?

More machetes, axes, and knives, to be sure. His own machete and Amio's knife were a beginning. Hato hoped eventually each of his wives and children would possess at least a machete, an axe and a knife. This would take time and work, for it was already clear the Tuan had no intention of showering these things as gifts. That was fine with Hato. He and his family were accustomed to work.

But was there something more? That the Tuan and his Nyonya intended to re-orient the Sawi universe was already clear, but Hato still could not guess what form that new universe would take. Yet he was burning with curiosity to learn more of their intentions.

"*Es aphaem ke hafem!* Let's go to the village!" he called, rising to his feet.

Cooking fires were extinguished with water sprinkled from bamboo cruses. Grass mats were rolled up. Memorial skulls of relatives were tied to rafters

172

to await a later return of the clan to the treehouse. Babies were fitted into carrying bags and swung onto their mothers' backs. Then the long procession descended the stairpoles to the waiting dugouts.

After an hour of paddling down the Tumdu's twisting course, Hato and his family approached the tributary's junction with the Kronkel. They could see the Tuan's little square house in its clearing, and to either side the various larger clearings in which the people of Kamur, Haenam and Yohwi had erected their temporary homes, preparatory to building more permanent dwellings later. Gray smoke curled lazily over the russet brown of newly dried thatch.

Suddenly Hato's one eye noticed that more than just smoke was arcing over the settlement. Shafts of white cane flashed like needles in the sun as they criss-crossed just above the treetops before falling back to earth. Just then a distant sound of shouting became audible. And wailing.

"Hurry!" Hato shouted. "There's a battle raging in the Tuan's yard!"

13

War at My Door

"Carol!" I shouted above the din that suddenly surrounded me. "Keep the baby away from the windows!"

Grabbing up my language notes I dashed toward the house, ducking in and out among the armed men who had suddenly appeared from the direction of Kamur. Meanwhile my Sawi language informant, Narai, vanished into the forest in the opposite direction.

As I ran, I looked in the direction of Haenam, where a second mass of angry men were already releasing arrows toward the attackers. I saw three of the arrows arcing high overhead and tried to guess their trajectory. They all seemed to be falling straight toward me, so I leaped behind our house and under the shelter of the roof. One, two, three, they sliced into the ground within a forty-foot radius of our home. Not as close as I had expected.

A steady rattling of vine bowstrings mixed with the outcry of battle as I climbed the back steps on the lee side of our home and hurried inside. Carol, heeding my warning, had caught Stephen up from his afternoon nap and taken him to our storeroom, where an interior wall would help to impede any random arrow that might come in through a screen window or a gap in the exterior walls of our home. While Carol stayed beside Stephen, I went to the front door and looked out.

Most of the men of Kamur were now spread out across the open ground we had cleared between our home and the Kronkel. Others had taken up positions on the far side of the little shelter I had been using for language study. The advance guard of Haenam were stretched out in a long line on the far side of an intervening swampy area. No one was trying to hide behind anything. It was obvious they preferred to fight in the clear.

Those who had brought spears to the battle thrust them point up in the ground, freeing their hands for their bows. Fixing the enemy with a deadly glare, they began to weave from side to side, stretching to full height to release an arrow, crouching again to provide as small a target as possible, leaping to avoid the lightning shafts flashing toward them. Their absorption in the lethal business was total—with arrows volleying at speeds in excess of one hundred miles per hour, even a split second's inattention could be fatal.

The more experienced fighters formed the frontal lines on each side, shooting and dodging at a range of about fifty yards. The less experienced, most of them teen-age boys, stood further back, lofting their arrows high in the air to rain on the enemy position from above. Thus each combatant, while compelled to give his full attention to the shafts coming toward him with greater force and accuracy at near ground level, labored also under the unnerving prospect of being struck in the head or shoulders by a barbtip falling from above. As each man exhausted the supply of arrows he had brought with him, he simply grabbed others lodged in the ground around him and fired them back at the enemy.

In the background of both sides of the battle, women waved their sago-pounding sticks threateningly, shouting curses at the enemy over the heads of their menfolk, stamping their feet in rage or wailing in apprehension. Still further back, children climbed up on logs or stumps of trees to improve their view of the spectacle.

Tension soared as combatants and spectators alike waited for the first arrow to strike human flesh, knowing that as soon as one man was hit, his enemies would immediately concentrate a volley of arrows directly at him, hoping to inflict still more wounds upon him while he was momentarily distracted or disabled. Determined not to be that first man, the numerous antagonists maneuvered with reflexes sharpened to the limits of human acuity.

I moved out onto the front porch, full of adrenalin and poised for action, yet benumbed with indecision.

It took a few seconds for one thought to get through: *This is real.* Condition yourself, man, you're not watching a cinema, nor are you dreaming.

Those are real men and they're really trying to kill each other. Every one of them is dangling like a tempting morsel over the hungry maw of death. Right now one of these living, breathing personalities you've just begun to interact with may be snuffed out for eternity. Just when you're getting ready to share the message they've never heard.

Act, man! Do something! But while you're doing it, don't let yourself forget—*this is for real!*

I moved forward to the head of the stairs. I opened my mouth to shout at them to stop, but then I hesitated. If I shouted, I might distract someone just when an arrow was coming straight at him. I could be a secondary cause of someone getting wounded or killed.

Maybe it would be better to just run out there waving my arms. Surely they would all stop shooting then. Surely they know if they kill me, the horizon is not crowded with Tuans waiting to come in and take my place. On the other hand, maybe winning this battle means more to them than having a Tuan around.

Then an echo of advice someone had given me came back: "Be careful about trying to act the peace-maker—it takes only one arrow in the right place, and your ministry, if not your life, will be ended."

That's right, I thought. Look at those men—they know how to handle themselves down there among those flying arrows. I don't. Probably if I just pray and wait no one will get hurt. Surely God doesn't expect me to intervene when I don't even know the lang. . . .

A mighty shout rocked the arena. Haenam thought one of their arrows had struck Tumo, but their whoop of exultation was premature. At the last split second Tumo had leaped in the air, the arrow passing under his thigh. Tumo, one of those whose salvation I had yearned for in my dream.

Emotion welled up within me as Haenam tried to take advantage of Tumo's temporary loss of balance, sending arrow after arrow speeding toward him. If they kill him, I reasoned, Kamur will not give up until they even the score. It is crucial that this battle be stopped before blood is shed!

"Blessed are the peacemakers," a voice within me seemed to whisper, "for they shall be called the children of God." Peacemaking *is* one of my tasks, I concluded, and what basis do I have to expect such a profound obligation to be easy, painless, riskless? Perhaps every genuine act of peacemaking must of necessity entail risk for the peacemaker.

Besides, the real battle here is not between Kamur and Haenam—it is between this savagery and my gospel. Everything I do among these people establishes a precedent. If I just stand here I'll be setting a precedent of noninvolvement. I need to set a clear precedent now at the beginning, a precedent I can gradually reinforce and strengthen in days to come.

I leaped from the steps shouting that handiest of all the Sawi words I would ever learn: "*Es!* That's enough!" Crouching low and praying hard, I moved closer to Kamur's end of the field of fire, waving at Haenam to stop shooting. The firing stopped on the flank of the battle nearest me, but still continued in the center and on the far side. Taking courage, I moved in closer still. Some of the men on both sides tried to wave me back, but I kept inching closer.

I could feel charisma from God rushing through me. Disconcerted, the Kamur men moved toward the river to draw Haenam's fire away from my position, but I had already interrupted the momentum of the battle. Its crescendo had passed. I was suffused with joy.

The shooting ceased, and in its place shouting broke out on all sides. Men began to wave their bows rather than draw them. They were all still plenty angry, however.

Now that I had interrupted the shooting, how could I settle whatever grievance had caused the fighting in the first place? Clearly the same quarrel could flare up again if some civil settlement were not provided. Now words were needed, and there I stood wordless at the edge of the throng.

A strong hand gripped my left elbow. I turned and found myself looking into Hato's one eye, and it was very stern. His chest was heaving. "Tuan," he seemed to be saying, "you wait back here. I'll take care of this."

I heaved a sigh of relief as he strode past me and planted himself in front of the Kamur warriors, his back turned fearlessly toward Haenam. Raising his voice above the din he began to chide his friends in thundering Sawi. Restrained, the men of Kamur lowered their weapons.

Haenam, however, was still in a foment of rage. Surely, I thought, there must be someone over there I can appeal to. I quickly skirted around the swamp to Haenam's position, searching for someone . . . anyone.

Then I saw Hadi standing on a stump with his arms folded, calmly watching the proceedings. Hadi! Of course!

"Hadi!" I roared, groping for words. "You . . . you TALK!"

For a moment he gaped as if stunned by my command, then he leaped from the stump and placed himself directly in front of the Haenam mob, shouting them down with his marvelous voice.

Joining three villages into one was an experiment the Sawi had tried only rarely in living memory—it was the kind of experiment that so readily ended in bloodshed! Even the recent attempt to join just two villages together at the far end of the *kidari* had ended in the battle which cost Hato his right eye. Little wonder Sawi communities preferred to leave several miles of empty jungle as buffer zones separating them from even their fondest neighbors.

In the present case, the strong inducement which had drawn Kamur, Haenam, and Yohwi together was the novelty and practicality—and perhaps a certain prestige—of living beside two extremely rare beings believed to be a source of potentially limitless supplies of axes, machetes, knives, razor blades, mirrors, fishline, fishhooks and who knew what else! The people of Kamur knew they had a right to live beside the Tuan for the obvious reason that he had chosen to build his home on their land! Haenam and Yohwi likewise claimed proximity rights because they had made first contact with him.

And so they had agreed to share, to experiment. During the three days it had taken for me to return from Kawem with Carol and Stephen, the men who had helped me build my home had decided they would bring *their* wives and children also, gathering them out of the deep sago swamps where they normally lived. Working together as whole families, they had hastily erected *saurai,* "temporary" houses on the ground. These they would use as shelters while they celebrated our arrival, and also while they erected permanent *anep,* "high" houses before the monsoon rains flooded the swamps.

Thus we were delighted when, after that first drum-shattered night among the Sawi, the light of a new day revealed the evidence that three entire villages intended to reside permanently around us. We knew this would greatly facilitate our interaction with the tribe, and also increase our ability to provide the medical help they so desperately needed.

For the better part of three days and nights the entire populace had continued their drum-beating, singing and dancing—save for one memorable interruption when the MAF float plane returned for its second landing on the Kronkel, bringing, among other things, a small radio transmitter, our only means of immediate communication with the outside world. Once the marathon celebration ended, most of the people had, like Hato, returned to their jungle dwellings to gather supplies of food prior to beginning work on their permanent homes at the new village site.

It was now about a week since our arrival, and the people had just returned from the jungle in good spirits, their canoes laden with fresh provisions—but almost immediately the camaraderie they had enjoyed during the three days of dancing had vanished as Kamur and Haenam clashed in front of our home. We marveled at how quickly their attitudes could change.

Prospects for the future of our newly assembled community looked grim indeed. If only we could restrain them from actual bloodshed until we had time to learn their language, we thought, then perhaps we could hold the three villages together.

It was to prove a futile hope.

14

The Tuan Eats Brains

The cluster of curious Sawi boys crept slowly closer to the lighted window, venturing where formerly only elders of the tribe had dared to approach. At first the Tuan's lamp both blinded them with its glare and unnerved them with its hissing, but gradually their eyes became accustomed, their courage steady.

They looked inside. Only the sago-frond walls were familiar. Everything else, from the lamp itself to the glowing yellow curtains, could hardly seem more alien. Counters, a table, chairs, tablecloth, plates and bowls, knives, forks and spoons, pictures on the wall, a kerosene-burning stove were all strangely puzzling to the inquisitive swamp urchins.

Clinging together for moral support, they watched the Tuan and the Nyonya sit down with their baby. They observed closely as the Tuan lifted a steaming bowl of food and began serving some of it onto his plate, their eyes growing wide with mingled fascination and horror. They glanced at each other and trembled.

Then one of them put into words what they were all thinking, *"Asem mohop ke manken!"*

Abruptly they bolted from the porch and fled through the darkness to Kamur village, spreading with hushed tones an incredible report from house to house. From inside various longhouses, the elders called back to them, "You must be mistaken!"

"Go quick and see for yourselves!" the boys urged.

Their curiosity aroused, the elders of Kamur thronged immediately to the Tuan's front porch. Looking up, we saw just the whites of their eyes gleaming out of the blackness. We greeted them, but they did not respond. Their eyes were riveted upon the food we were eating.

"It's true!" one of them exclaimed in words unintelligible to us. "It's true indeed! The Tuan *is* eating brains!"

Wondering what the excitement was all about, I lifted another forkful of macaroni to my lips.

As I was about to turn out the lamp for the night, we heard the sound of a woman crying in great distress. Taking a flashlight, I picked my way among stumps and roots toward Kamur's smoke-haloed longhouses.

"Why is that woman crying?" I called from the edge of the village.

A man named Asyman looked out of the doorway

of his home and tried to wave me away. I stood my ground and asked again, "Why is that woman crying?"

Asyman replied with words I did not understand, except for the last one, *"Amynahai!* Go away!"

Others also were now standing in their doorways waving me away. The woman, meanwhile, stopped crying.

Feeling somewhat self-conscious over my apparently unwelcome intrusion, as well as my inability to understand their explanations, I finally returned home, still none the wiser. From time to time, before we fell asleep we heard the woman cry out again. Then just before daybreak we were awakened by loud wailing from Kamur.

In the morning we learned that the woman, Maso, died giving birth to twins. The twins also died. Even if they had both lived, their own father would have killed one of them, in line with Sawi belief that the second twin born is actually an evil spirit trying to invade the community by impersonating a truly human child and being born along with it. In the demon-pervaded world of the Sawi, not even the womb of a mother is safe from satanic intrusion.

Sorrowing with the Sawi over Maso's death, we groaned with longing for the day when the Sawi would realize we could help them even in such private matters as childbirth, and would trust us to give what help we could.

Carol was trying to train Haimai as a houseboy.

After he had dutifully filled our gasoline-powered washing machine with steaming hot water, she showed him how to add soapsuds. Then, while gathering clothes for the washing, she happened to see a used teabag lying by the sink. She handed it to Haimai, telling him in broken Sawi to take it out and throw it in the garbage can. Looking confused, he carried the teabag outside.

A few minutes later Carol called me to start the washing machine engine. Once the engine was running, she pulled the lever to start the agitator. Just as she was about to plunge the first load of laundry into the churning suds, she gasped, "Don, what are all those black specks in my nice clean washwater?"

I dipped out a handful of suds and examined the black specks. Tca leaves!

Earlier in the day, the tall Atohwaem named Yakub had announced his intention to take the widow Fasaha as his third wife. One end of Haenam was in favor of the transaction, but Nair in the other end of the village protested that the widow should be given to him instead.

At midday, when Fasaha's relatives decided against his proposal, Nair, supported by his brother Paha, stormed out of his house shouting threats at Yakub. Two of Yakub's friends, Mavu and Sinar, came out to face the two furious men. The four rapidly closed in combat, while the shrieking of their womenfolk rose like a warning siren above the village.

The fight lasted only a few seconds. Mavu was

first to strike. Lunging in with his *kafam,* a multiple-warhead spear featuring a cluster of barbed points bound together with vine, he impaled Paha in the hip. Nair, seeing his brother trailing a stream of blood, launched a bamboo-bladed pig arrow at Sinar. The shaft sliced easily through the muscle of Sinar's upper arm and even penetrated a short distance into his rib cage. Mavu in turn retaliated by burying the entire blade of a pig arrow in Nair's thigh.

When I arrived on the scene, Mavu was still raging but there was no one left to answer his challenge in the blood-stained village clearing. Seeing the extent of the wounds, I called to Carol to bring bandages and penicillin, while I stood by to make sure Mavu did not try to take further advantage of his two opponents in their weakened condition. Our hands were stained with blood by the time we finished cleaning and binding wounds and giving injections of penicillin.

As we were leaving, I gazed straight into Mavu's eyes, burning with desire to say something to him, but what could I say? I knew if I upbraided him for nearly killing two men, he would only shrug his shoulders as if to say, "So what?" So instead I said cryptically, "You have made my wife's hands bloody."

The remark took him by surprise. He glanced quickly at Carol's hands and a sudden realization of the inappropriateness of the scene he had helped to create seemed to startle him. Mavu winced, fearing he had unwittingly committed some dark impropriety of cosmic consequence.

I longed to tell him of Someone else's hands that

had been made bloody for his sake, and that with truly cosmic significance, but the words just weren't there. Not yet. So I had to leave him, as he would later confess, trembling inwardly.

With repeated injections of penicillin to prevent infection, the three patients recovered quickly from wounds that might otherwise have proved fatal. By keeping death at bay, we had again forestalled a blood feud which, once initiated, could have gone on for years. This time the danger had existed between opposing clans within Haenam village itself. An even greater concern was to forestall a blood feud on a larger scale between Haenam and Kamur.

With this sense of the life-and-death urgency of our task heavy upon us, we decided to delay building our permanent home for one year, in order to launch an all-out campaign to crack the code of the Sawi language in the shortest possible time. With a few improvements here and there, and careful use of space, the little twenty-by-twenty-foot "thatch-box" would prove livable enough, provided we could endure the armies of insects and other forms of wildlife which occasionally found their way under and over wall plates and through cracks in sago-frond walls.

We sprayed the piers supporting our home with residual spray which served to ward off invasions of termites and other kinds of crawling insects which require contact with ground moisture in order to survive. But flying insects such as cockroaches, crickets, flies and mosquitoes waged a constant campaign of harassment against us and our basic supplies.

Certain varieties of wildlife seemed to be in league with each other. For example, under cover of darkness, crickets would eat holes in our mosquito nets, allowing mosquitoes laden with debilitating payloads of malarial parasites, dengue viruses or filarial larvae to penetrate our defences. Rats also would chew holes in plastic food containers, enabling hordes of ants and cockroaches to spoil the contents.

We were not without our allies, however. Tiny jumping spiders and iridescent green lizards haunted our walls and window screens, hunting flies by day, mosquitoes and moths by night. In addition, hordes of night birds and bats flitted around our home each evening, devouring mosquitoes and moths drawn to our home by the lamp.

At certain times of the year hordes of flying ants would hatch by the thousands in the jungle around us and then converge upon our home as soon as the lamp was lit at dusk. Swarming into our brightly lit living room, they would first dash themselves against the lamp glass and then rain down stunned or dying to cover the pages of a book as one of us read, or to clog the keys of the typewriter as one of us worked. They would get tangled in our hair or tickle their way up our shirt sleeves.

They helped us develop the habit of retiring early.

My goal each day was to gain ten hours of exposure to the Sawi language. This included three or four hours of interaction with language informants, strug-

gling to isolate new words, phrases and grammatical constructions. I devoted the rest of the time to visiting the Sawi homes or manhouses, traveling with them to the jungle or to other villages, listening to their conversation by the river in the evening, trying to enter in with meaningful questions and responses.

With no interpreters to help us, we often had to track down the meaning of words by sheer guessing. I step on a pole and it breaks. A Sawi exclaims, *"Getar haser!" Haser* I already know means "not," so I guess that *getar* means "strong," and the man is saying the pole I stepped on is "not strong."

To check this, I point to something else that is not strong and describe it as *getar haser.*

My informant may agree, replying, *"Esawab! O tai getar haser—inapi!"*

I then will hazard guesses that *esawab* means "true," *o tai* means "that also," and *inapi* means "weak." The total utterance, by this theory, emerges as, "True! That also is not strong—it is weak!"

This approach was tenuous at best, especially in the early stages when we had so few clues to guide our guessing. Often a confused look or an incredulous outburst of laughter would tell us it was time to backtrack and try another guess.

Once, while learning to paddle standing up in a narrow Sawi dugout, I lost my balance and fell in. My Sawi escort shook his head sadly and said, *"Tuan, go nigi kabi mar jah!"*

I guessed that he was saying, "You should have leaned the other way!" or "Watch out for crocodiles!" But months later when I returned to my notes, I realized that he had said, "Tuan, you have a bad relationship with our canoes!"

Day by day, word by word, we enlarged our linguistic beachhead. Eventually, we discovered the Sawi words for "joyful," "sad," "stubborn," "foolish" and "angry." We could now describe emotions!

Later, with the aid of other Sawi words that meant "think," "repent," "forgive," "to judge," and "love," we began to penetrate into the language's inner sanctum of abstract expression. We were ranging more freely . . . gaining confidence . . . getting ready. The nirvana of total communication looked a little closer.

Or was it really just as far away as ever?

15

Meeting in the Manhouse

The tattered remnants of an all-night rainstorm were still scudding above the ironwood trees, as I slowly approached the Haenam-Yohwi manhouse, notes in hand, walking in an early morning world of puddles, drips and luminous mist.

The manhouse stood apart by the river, a grim guardian of the twin rows of longhouses recently erected by the people of Haenam and Yohwi. To an outsider, a manhouse appears little different from the usual Sawi dwelling—just a longhouse that somehow got left out of line, with perhaps a few human and animal skulls festooning its doorposts to indicate the prowess of its occupants.

But to the Sawi eye, a manhouse is no mere dwelling. It is the Parthenon of Sawi culture. A banquet hall for honoring distinguished guests. A think-tank for hatching schemes of war. A forum for oratory, ribald humor or strident boasting. A covert for occasional homosexual liaisons. A slaughterhouse for cannibalistic feasts.

I planned to make it an Areopagus for proclaiming the Son of the living God. A portal through which the gospel would eventually reach every smoky fireplace in the longhouses of Haenam and Yohwi. But it would not happen without a struggle.

The first obstacle was language. Speaking Sawi was proving far more than an exercise in stringing simple terms together. Often a single word turned out to be only a stem to which a seemingly limitless number of suffixes or chains of suffixes could be attached.

Each verb, for example, has nineteen tenses in its indicative mood alone. So far I had isolated the functions of only one-third of those nineteen tenses. Also, each of the nineteen tenses occurred in both a first-person and a non-first-person form, making a total of thirty-eight verb endings to choose from every time I wanted to make a simple indicative statement in Sawi.

Another group of verb endings were slowly emerging as the subjunctive mood of the language, a system for expressing "if," "could have," "would have," and "should have." Further, I was getting glimmerings of an imperative mood, a brace of suffixes which say "let me," "let us," "let him," as well as give commands in the second person.

Apparently concrete verb stems became etymological phantoms which could assume any one of fifteen different shapes even before one began extending them with suffixes. One form of the stem proclaimed the subject as singular, another as plural. Still others indicated action aimed at either a singular or plural object. Other forms signified operations which were either customary, progressive, repeated, reciprocal, experimental, conclusive, partial, excessive or obstructed.

In Sawi, every sequence has to be in correct time order with no steps omitted. The grammar is correspondingly set up to handle long action sequences in a smooth, flowing manner.

Every statement has to be classified as either firsthand or secondhand information. Sawi won't let you take credit for someone else's thoughts. Nor will it let you avoid responsibility for your own utterances. It abhors indistinctness. It tolerates no nonsense. It would resist a translation of *Alice in Wonderland* like oil resists water. Surgically precise, transistorized description is its goal.

Sometimes I felt like my brain circuits would get shorted before I mastered Sawi. And yet learning it was a great adventure. I often felt like a mathematician must feel as he tackles problems and breaks through into new formulas which work like magic.

Sawi is so enchantingly specific in its vocabulary. In English you open your eyes, your heart, a door, a tin can or someone's understanding, all with one humdrum verb "open." But in Sawi you *fagadon* your eyes, *anahagkon* your heart, *tagavon* a door, *tarifan* a tin can, and *dargamon* a listener's understanding.

If someone had shown me a statement of Sawi

grammar and asked me to guess the type of persons who developed it, I would have guessed a race of pedantist-philosopher types obsessed with fastidious concern for handling masses of detail efficiently.

And yet, looking deeper, I would have guessed they were also poets—an entire subclass of Sawi verbs is devoted to personifying inanimate objects as speaking! If a flower has a pleasant scent, it is saying *fok! fok!* to your nostrils. Is it also beautiful? It is saying *ga! ga!* to your eyes. When a star twinkles it is whispering *sevair! sevair!* If your eyes twinkle they are calling *si! si!* If mud squishes around your feet, it is murmuring *sos! sos!* In the Sawi universe, not only man, but all things are communicating.

Climbing up a notched pole, I entered the man-house and sat down on a grass mat among the men of Haenam and Yohwi. They didn't look like the philosopher-poets their language suggested they were. I felt I was sitting in the presence of a mystery. How did a culture addicted to barbarism develop such a refined, logical and efficient language? Perhaps the swift thought and keen reflexes needed to survive in a violent context served to produce linguistic efficiency also.

Or was their language an artifact pointing back to an earlier age of more complex aspirations? I had already noticed that the Sawi had a deep, almost compulsive esteem for their ancestors. Perhaps there was more than just a sentimental basis for it.

For a few minutes I sat quietly among them, conditioning myself anew to the strangeness of the men with whom I must communicate, and to the brooding atmosphere of the manhouse itself, with its gloomy-eyed skulls, weapons, grass mats, flickering fires, and cobwebs heavy with congealed smoke.

In spite of the many aspects of their lives which made me shudder, it was impossible not to respect the men around me. Every one of them was an accomplished naturalist, versed from childhood in the names and ways of hundreds of species of flora and fauna. Any one of them could survive independently in a wilderness where I, cut off from outside help, would waste away.

They were obviously men of great courage and strong wills. They could move easily through a rain of arrows or risk disembowelment from the tusks of horrendous wild boars. Even more remarkable, they could transform a seemingly hostile wilderness into a bountiful supermarket where goods were free for the taking without destroying the wilderness in the process.

Basically, there were two presuppositions I shared with the Sawi—belief in a supernatural world and in the importance of interaction between that supernatural world and men. The Sawi believed in a hierarchy of disinterested, if not malicious, demons and departed spirits of the dead. I trusted in an infinite yet personal God who loves justice and mercy.

The Sawi were convinced that no misfortune happened by accident, but was invariably caused by demons who could be either activated or restrained by witchcraft. I was persuaded that all things were either commanded or permitted by a divine Providence which in turn could be influenced by prayer.

Beyond this point, there was little common viewpoint in our respective world views. Here was a barrier even greater than that of language. Somehow I must bridge the gulf in a meaningful way.

I laid out a few notes on the mat in front of me and started in. First I coined a name for God in Sawi—*Myao Kodon*, "the greatest Spirit." Then I tried to describe Him. I explained that He didn't live in just one submerged log or one sago palm, like Sawi *hamars*, but instead filled the whole sky and the whole earth.

"In fact," I added, "we're sitting here inside Him right now!"

They looked around involuntarily, startled at the thought.

"In the case of *hamars*," I continued, "you use witchcraft to keep them from entering your villages, your homes, your very bodies. But there is no charm, no fetish that can keep *Myao Kodon* away. He respects no witchcraft. He is everywhere and no one can ever get away from Him."

A look of defenselessness crossed several faces.

"And because everything—the sun, the moon, the weather, rivers, jungle, animals and people—are all inside Him, He knows all about everything. He knows what everyone is saying, doing and thinking. We cannot see Him, but He sees us!

"He also controls everything, just as easily as you

control the movements of your own muscles. Without Him the wind cannot blow, nor the rain fall. The sun cannot shine, nor the moon rise without His power. Neither could plants grow, nor babies be conceived without His provision."

Kani and others leaned forward, listening. Previously they had received only hardware from the outside world. Now they were hearing ideas. They seemed excited.

As I continued, a man named Gar came and sat facing me. After absorbing each sentence, he turned to his fellows and carefully repeated what I said. Often he rephrased my words into clearer Sawi, adding interpretive comments of his own—some of which were humorously far astray.

It was a mark of politeness, and at first I found it disconcerting, but later I became profoundly thankful for this custom. Listening to Gar rephrase my thoughts gave me priceless insights into the Sawi mind. It also allowed me time to work out the syntax for my next sentence. More important, every time Gar repeated what I said, he was steadily reinforcing the message in a way which did not create boredom.

Line by line, I expanded the contrast between the petty, cynical spirits whose dread shadow lay over every aspect of Sawi life, and the infinite creative God whose love for justice and mercy has involved Him in a profoundly sacrificial pursuit of lost men. I wanted to give them a wide, clear basis for making a free choice between those spirits and God. Some of the men seemed disinterested. Others listened in open-jawed amazement, as if startled to hear their language express concepts which they, the owners of the language, had never dreamed of.

I spoke of God creating man in the midst of a beauteous, bountiful world, the advent of evil into the human community, the age-old promise of a Deliverer, and finally the wondrous appearance of that Deliverer. I was approaching the climax of my narrative, describing the ministry of Jesus among the Jewish people, when suddenly Maum yawned out loud and reached for his knife and a piece of split vine lying on the mat beside him.

Gripping one end of the vine between his toes, he pulled it taut and began trimming it with his knife. He was making a new bowstring. He seemed to have tuned out completely.

Others likewise resumed little conversations of their own. I sensed that if I had been talking about the Asmat, the Kayagar, or the Auyu instead of the Jews, they would have kept on listening. At any rate, I had reached the end of their attention span. Whoever the Jews were, they sounded awfully far away.

On subsequent visits I expanded further on the life and ministry of Jesus, trying to establish His reality and relevance to their lives, but without apparent success. The Sawi were not accustomed to projecting their minds into cultures and settings so forbiddingly dissimilar from their own.

Only once did my presentation win a ringing response from them. I was describing Judas Iscariot's betrayal of the Son of God. About halfway through the description I noticed they were all listening intently. They noted the details: for three years Judas had kept close company with Jesus, sharing the same food, traveling the same road.

That any associate of Jesus would have conceived the idea of betraying such an impressive figure was highly unlikely. And if anyone *had* conceived the idea, one of Jesus' inner circle of trusted disciples would have been the least likely to choose such a course. And yet Judas, one of Jesus' disciples, had chosen to betray Him and carried out the dreadful act alone, without any of the other disciples suspecting his plot.

At the climax of the story, Maum whistled a birdcall of admiration. Kani and several others touched their fingertips to their chests in awe. Still others chuckled.

At first I sat there confused. Then the realization broke through. *They were acclaiming Judas as the hero of the story!* Yes, Judas, the one whom I had portrayed as the satanically motivated enemy of truth and goodness!

A feeling of coldness gripped my spine. I tried to protest that Jesus was good. He was the Son of God, the Saviour. It was evil to betray Him. But nothing I said would erase that gleam of savage enjoyment from their eyes.

Kani leaned forward and exclaimed, "That was real *tuwi asonai man!*"

Whatever *tuwi asonai man* meant.

I got up and left the manhouse, oppressed with a feeling of hopelessness. I looked across the swamp to the little home we had built. It looked like a monument to futility. Carol was dispensing medicine from the porch, while Stephen played on a mat behind her. Was this the limit of the good we could

do for the Sawi? Bringing health to their physical bodies while the core of their beings remained remote and unreachable?

The men were still discussing the story and laughing over it as I headed home. Alone in my study, I began to pray. But as I prayed, Kani's mysterious phrase kept going through my mind. After a while, I took a pen and wrote the strange expression on a three-by-five card.

Tuwi asonai man! Its basic parts were simple enough. *Tuwi* means "pig." *Ason* is "to catch," and with the *-ai* ending, "having caught." *Man* means simply "to do."

"Having caught a pig, to do. . . ." To do what?

I went to the door and called one of my language informants, Narai. When he arrived I asked him to explain *tuwi asonai man.* Narai looked through the window and pointed with his chin to a young pig which Hato had earlier captured in the jungle. Tamed, it was now roaming freely around the village yard.

"Tuan, when Hato first caught that pig, he kept it in his own home, fed it by hand, and protected it from the village dogs. Now that it is roaming about, he still throws down scraps of food for it every day. The pig feels secure, protected, well-fed. He is free to come and go as he pleases. But one day when the pig is mature, what will happen to it?"

"Hato and his family will butcher and eat it," I replied.

"But does the pig have any warning now of that coming event?"

"Not the slightest."

"Right!" Narai agreed. *Tuwi asonai man* means to do with a man as Hato is doing with that pig—*to fatten him with friendship for an unsuspected slaughter!*

Narai sat watching the effect of his words working on my countenance.

"Does this actually happen?" I asked naively.

"Indeed it does," he replied quickly, and began to relate the account of a stranger who used to visit Haenam frequently. On his first visit, he had been feasted royally, flattered with praise, and invited to return again and again. The story ended when the man's patrons became his butchers, the fed became food.

Narai continued with the story of Kani's and Mahaen's treachery against Mahaen's relatives in Wasohwi. The conclusion left me sitting in astonished silence.

"But if Mahaen committed a crime like that," I ventured, "why is he such a popular man? Why have so many men promised their daughters in marriage to him?"

The look in Narai's eyes told me he just didn't see the point of my question. And that was an answer in itself.

As Narai continued relating still other examples of classic Sawi treachery, I was thinking hard. I saw now that the Sawi were not only cruel, but *honored* cruelty. Their highest pleasure depended upon the misery and despair of others. They had long ago passed beyond what they would consider a layman's concept of murder into a far-out life-style where treachery was idealized as a virtue, a goal of life.

Overt killing no longer held real pleasure for them. They would even risk letting an intended victim escape in order to pursue the more sophisticated ideal expressed in *tuwi asonai man*. That was why the story of Judas Iscariot had aroused them. It had touched the core of their psyche, awakening a deep, almost subliminal response.

Judas was a super-Sawi! And Christ the object of Judas' treachery meant nothing to the men in the manhouse.

My task was to reverse that situation totally. On the basis of Scripture, there could be no compromise, no easy counting of converts who still harbored this tragic philosophy. But how could one man and his wife reverse the world view of an entire people, a world view which had already been entrenched in their collective psyche for perhaps thousands of years?

I knew deep inside that mere recitation of the gospel would not be enough. Nor would I resort to the "schooling" method used by some, in which one simply writes off the present generation as unteachable, concentrating instead on enrolling hundreds of children in schools, where a steady Christian influence over many years aims at a second- or third-generation victory.

I wanted to win *this* generation of Sawi. And I wanted to win them on their own ground and by their own fireplaces. If the gospel could not win men like Mahaen, Kani, Hato and Kigo, it was not the message it claimed to be.

I was game, but I was also stymied. I didn't know

how to tackle a cultural enigma like this. I headed home for lunch, groaning inwardly. "Lord, in all of time and space has Your message ever encountered a world view more opposite than this one? Could there be a world view more opposite to the gospel? And has any man ever faced a communication problem bigger than this one You've assigned to me?"

Take John the Baptist. His communication problem was a cinch compared to mine. He preached a baptism of repentance for the forgiveness of sins to a people already acquainted with the rite of baptism and with concepts like repentance and forgiveness of sins.

He proclaimed the coming of Messiah to a people who had been waiting thousands of years for Messiah to appear! And when Messiah appeared, John had only to shout one sentence and every Hebrew within hearing was made aware of the purpose of Messiah's coming: "Behold the Lamb of God who takes away the sin of the world!"

John shouted it once, waited a day, and then said a second time, "Behold the Lamb of God!" His communication was so effective two of his own disciples left him immediately and followed Jesus!

From hoary history, the lamb sacrifice had been an integral part of Hebrew culture. Something the people were already intellectually and emotionally committed to. But the Sawi had never heard of a lamb, nor, as far as I could tell, had they ever entertained the thought of an innocent substitute dying for the sin of the guilty.

Consider the case of Jesus Himself. On the surface, one would think anyone embarking on a ministry as unique as His would face a tremendous communication barrier. In actual fact, He enjoyed the same communication advantage John the Baptist had exploited before Him.

For Nicodemus, Jesus likened Himself to the serpent of brass which Moses once hoisted on a pole, so Hebrews then dying of snakebite could look at it and be healed. Nicodemus could hardly miss the point. Jesus is the object of faith to whom we must all look or else we perish.

For Nathaniel, He likened Himself to the ladder the patriarch Jacob saw in a dream, the ladder with angels of God going up and down on it. Nathaniel could hardly miss the point: Jesus is the means of communication between God and man.

For a Jewish multitude seeking miraculous supplies of food, He became the true manna from heaven, saying, "Moses gave you not the bread from heaven. . . . The Bread of God is He who comes down from heaven and gives life to the world."

Clearly, a great deal of groundwork had already been done to prepare Hebrews to recognize their Messiah. The sovereign God had laid that groundwork millenniums before by incubating within Hebrew culture scores of redemptive analogies pointing forward to Him. John the Baptist and Jesus made a dramatic impact by explaining who was the perfect, personal fulfillment of those redemptive analogies. They had, after all, been placed there millenniums earlier to be exploited at the right moment and in this very manner!

The gospel, coming as a message from another

world, achieved its first ethnic conquest, not only by the demonstration of miracles, but even more significantly, by dynamic appropriation of Hebrew redemptive analogies. It had been God's chosen strategy for introducing the Christ.

By that strategy John the Baptist's communication problem, and that of Jesus and His apostles, had been reduced to a minimum. Then came the writer of the New Testament letter to the Hebrews to develop that strategy in still greater depth.

And even when the gospel came to the Greeks, John the Apostle was able to introduce Christ to them as the *Logos*, lifting a term right out of their own Hellenistic philosophy: "In the beginning was the *Logos*, and the *Logos* was with God, and the *Logos* was God! . . . The *Logos* became flesh and dwelt among us."

But to me, as I gazed wistfully across the swamp toward the Haenam manhouse, it seemed that God had not troubled Himself to prepare the Sawi in any similar way for the coming of the gospel. Hebrews . . . yes! Greeks . . . yes! And even my own Anglo-Saxon forefathers were found with the pagan term *god*, a term which someone kindly appropriated to teach us something better than worshiping trees and rocks.

But the Sawi had no name for God. Nor even the concept of Him. No lamb sacrifice to teach the need for an atonement. No redemptive analogy I could use.

It looked as though God had led me to the end of the earth and left me alone to grapple with a communication problem greater than any He had ever required prophets or apostles to face. Or was I misreading the situation?

Surely His grace would find a way to break through to the Sawi also. There must be a way, but what could it be? "Lord," I prayed aloud as I walked along. "I need Your help!"

Carol listened with concern as I explained the nature of our problem over our lunch. "Do you think there's any chance they're. . . ."

". . . fattening *us* with friendship for a slaughter?" I said. "Quite likely the thought has crossed their minds, but the fact that we are their only source of steel axes probably weighs heavily in our favor, at least for the time being. My main concern is, how do we crack this idealization of treachery before it cracks us?"

"God always has a way," Carol said meaningfully. "There must be a way."

I agreed that if Jesus were physically present in that Haenam manhouse, He would not be stymied. Even if there was only one solution, He would find it unerringly. But Jesus was not there in physical manifestation.

There was only a man and a woman who hoped to qualify as His representatives, who trusted that the Spirit of Jesus was living and working in them. So that Spirit would have to reveal to them the same key their Lord would have used, or else there was no hope.

212

Reduced to utter dependence upon God, we set ourselves to *hope* for that key. We could not guess what form it would take. We only knew that it would be from God and would have His blessing.

The next day, really serious fighting broke out again between Haenam and Kamur.

16

Crisis by the Kronkel

In most cultures, training for war, if required, does not begin until the teen-age years. Among the Sawi, training for war begins in early childhood.

I have often seen a father keep repeating a command to a three- or four-year-old son while the child ignores his father as if he were not there. Vainly the father will harangue and threaten—and then turn and boast to a friend that his son is truly *kwai*, "strong-willed." And the son hears his father's boast.

Every Sawi child knows that if he throws a violent enough tantrum, he will get his way. I have even seen young children who have not yet learned to swim throw themselves in the river to compel a parent or sibling to come running and pick them up.

On the rare occasion when a parent strikes a child

with real intent to punish, the child will often strike back, or at least throw himself into convulsive rage to bend the parent's will. The parent will accept this reaction, thus encouraging a similar response next time. Generally, punishing a child is frowned upon, and the reason given is *mesu furamake gani*, "in case you break his spirit." Call it discipline-in-reverse.

The Sawi child is trained to obtain his will by sheer force of violence and temper. He is goaded constantly to take *otaham*, "revenge," every time he is hurt or insulted. He has also the open example of his parents themselves as they carry out violent retaliation against everything that offends them, not to mention the constant recitation of stories and legends which exalt violence and treachery as traditional obligations.

The end product, after sixteen to eighteen years of such programming, is a young man with a fighting instinct so deeply engrained that sometimes even a natural concern for self-preservation cannot suppress it. And in primeval southwest New Guinea, children raised by any other standard would quickly become the legitimate prey of their enemies.

It is not surprising, then, that whole villages of such men will bristle with spears and arrows at the mere drop of a word. Nor was it surprising, since we lived among *three* villages of such men, that we counted fourteen battles fought within sight of our home during the first two months we lived among the Sawi. After that we lost count.

This did not include run-of-the-mill family quarrels when a husband, for example, would punish his wife

by shooting an arrow through her arm or through her leg. Or beat her across the back with a flaming faggot. Or force her to sit in a corner staring at the wall for days on end, striking her soundly every time she dared look around at her children or other relatives—a punishment, called *yukop hauhuyap,* usually inflicted on young wives whose eyes strayed too often in the direction of strange men.

We became accustomed to the almost daily sight of blood. To the drumming sound of feet hurrying to war. To the unified shouting of masses of angry men. To the rattle of bow-vines and the thud of clubs striking flesh. To the high-pitched screaming of women as they beat the frond walls of their long-houses with heavy sago digging sticks in thundering protest against some injustice.

Had the Sawi and other tribes like them developed twentieth century war technology along with their subliminal killer-psyche, they might have been the scourge of half the earth. Trying to restrain such a culture from violence and counter-violence was like trying to force several hundred computers to give responses exactly opposite to those for which they were programmed.

Occasionally I had a measure of success. Like the time Atae announced that he was claiming Samani's only wife as his own third wife, and if Samani didn't like it he could step up and be killed. I climbed up into Atae's home, sat down with him by his fireplace and started reasoning with him about the judgment of God that would await him if he wronged Samani in this way. Atae sat there blinking in amazement

217

as my words sank in. He had his bow and arrows ready across his lap, waiting for Samani to arrive for the showdown.

"If I, a Tuan, am happy with one wife, why do you need three?" I asked, using every kind of leverage I could think of. "Now that Jesus' words have come to you, you are more responsible than you were before. You will offend *Myao Kodon* terribly if you do this."

It worked. That haunting suspicion that perhaps the Tuan was linked with supernatural powers the Sawi had not yet discovered, plus the strong impression that the Tuan was not merely taking sides with Samani, but was also personally concerned for Atae's own good, won the day.

High noon arrived. Samani appeared, beside himself with fury. He was a thin, sickly man and would have been no match for Atae. To the astonishment of the village, Atae made a public oration retracting his earlier announcement. To save face, he made it clear he was changing his mind only "out of respect for Tuan Don." To my surprise, Atae and Samani soon became close friends. So also did Atae and I.

But it wasn't always that easy. There was the day our smiling friend Er nearly got himself killed. He had been making advances at a girl, when suddenly her father, uncles and brothers turned against him. Er had three arrows in his body before I could rescue him.

The MAF float plane was passing nearby, so I called pilot George Boggs and requested a medical flight to take Er to a mission hospital one hundred miles to the north, where the deeply embedded barb-tips could be removed by surgery. Within ten minutes the aircraft had landed on the Kronkel, and by that time I had persuaded all of Er's relatives to allow Er to be flown out for surgery.

Or I thought I had. But as George took off down the *kidari*, taking Er into the unknown, I heard a shout of rage behind me. Er's older brother, Ama, drawing his bow, had an arrow aimed at me.

"You have sent my brother away!" he screeched. "I'll never see my brother again!" Before he could release his arrow, a flying tackle of several Sawi men bore him to the ground and quickly disarmed him.

A week or so later, MAF returned Er to us, healthy and happy, proudly displaying the three arrowtips which had somehow been removed from his flesh "while he slept." He also told astounding tales of soaring mountain peaks, of ground covered with stones—a rarity in the swamps, and of friendly Dani (Christian) tribesmen who had welcomed him as if he were a brother.

Later I overheard Ama, the one who had threatened me, trying to make a deal with another Sawi, saying, "Let's you and I wound each other so we can both go where Er went!"

Ama was also the one who now precipitated the most serious fighting we had yet seen after five months beside the Kronkel. Taking offense because a Haenam youth called him "lizard-skin," Ama rallied the young men of Kamur and attacked Haenam.

Later the leading men of both villages also became involved, and this time it was clear they would not be turned aside until they had inflicted serious casualties on the opposite group.

For five months we had worked hard to forestall death by violence, not only for the lives involved, but also so our community of three villages might remain intact. We had bandaged dozens of bloody wounds, given hundreds of shots of penicillin, shouted till our throats were hoarse, prayed till our eyes were heavy with sleep, reasoned, cajoled, paid for emergency medical flights, and even interposed our own bodies as a final persuasion to break off hostilities. Yet still hatred between Haenam and Kamur kept swelling like an irresistible tide.

The imminent slaying of at least one person, followed by a dispersal of the three villages and the commencement of a long blood-feud, now seemed unavoidable. So daily I pleaded with the leading men of Haenam and Kamur to make peace, but they would not listen. Fortunately, Hadi's village, Yohwi, remained largely uninvolved.

Suddenly one day a new thought stopped me in my tracks. You keep urging them to make peace, I said to myself, on the assumption that peace is possible for these people. Peace, however, requires assurance of sincere good will on both sides.

But among the Sawi, where *tuwi asonai man* is a constant possibility, can there ever be assurance of sincere good will? Each side knows perfectly the other side's capacity for using friendship as a means of treachery. Each side knows also that at any time a

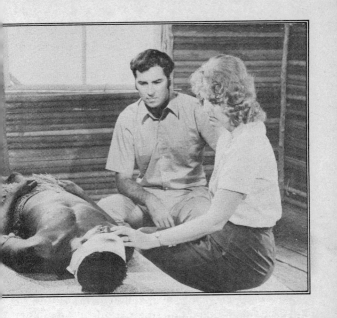

waness bind can be used to close the mouths of even those who normally would stand by a peace agreement.

Now I thought I saw why, when I urged them to make peace, they replied, "Tuan, you just don't understand!" Now I understood that when treachery is philosophically justified, true peace is impossible. Long, long ago the ancestors of the Sawi had locked the entire culture into a ceaseless treadmill of war.

Millenniums later, we had discovered the ancient treadmill still turning, the descendants still wearying themselves to keep from being ground under it. I wanted to let them off the treadmill. They had been on it long enough. But I could see no way.

The thing that puzzled me was why there were any Sawi left at all. With infant mortality higher than fifty percent, and an average life span probably lower than twenty-five years, they could hardly afford to kill each other in addition to the losses they suffered to the Asmat, the Kayagar, and disease. And yet they were bent on doing just that!

I concluded that possibly their habit of living in small, isolated groups had been the key to their survival. With potential enemies out of sight, there were fewer occasions to shed blood. Contagious diseases spread more slowly through a widely scattered population. People were more dependent on each other in small communities, and thus placed a higher premium on each other's lives. It was also easier for small groups to hide from outside enemies.

I concluded further that Carol and I had unintentionally deprived Haenam, Kamur and Yohwi of the mutual isolation they needed to survive in relative peace, by drawing them together into one community. It followed that for the good of the people, we ought to leave them. It would be a bitter pill to swallow, but I knew without us, they would scatter to their deep jungle homes and be at peace. In the meantime we could try to reach other Sawi communities to the north, hopefully returning later to minister to Haenam, Kamur and Yohwi individually on an itinerant basis.

Carol and I prayed together about this course of action, and then I went out to talk with the men in the manhouses of both Haenam and Kamur. "Since you cannot make peace with each other," I said, "it is clear to us that we ought to leave you. If we stay here, it is only a matter of time until men are killed, and then you will be locked in a blood-feud which may take still more lives.

"There are other Sawi villages over on the Au River—Tamor, Sato, Ero and Hahami—we will go and see if they are living at peace with each other and try to teach them."

My words touched off a tumult of discussion in both manhouses. I returned to Carol, wondering—will Haenam and Kamur angrily blame each other for our decision to leave, and launch fresh attacks? Or would both villages decide that if we would no longer be their source of medicine and steel axes, perhaps they could find other uses for us? As darkness fell, we could still hear discussion raging in both manhouses.

I was struggling against a dark Conradian despair,

compounded both by the realization that Carol, now pregnant with our second child, would find moving into another jungle home a very difficult task, and that Stephen, sick with malaria, was growing pale and listless.

I had just turned off the pressure lamp when I heard a shout outside our back door. I took a flashlight and walked out onto the back porch. My beam revealed the grim faces of a host of leading men from both warring factions—Kani, Mahaen, Maum, Hato, Kaiyo, Kigo and many others.

"Tuan," one of them pleaded solemnly, "don't leave us!"

"But I don't want you to kill each other," I replied.

"Tuan, we're not going to kill each other." The speaker paused, and steeled himself as he said, "Tuan, tomorrow we are going to make peace!"

17

Cool Water Tomorrow

"Make peace?" I echoed unbelievingly. For what the speaker actually said was, "Tomorrow we are going to sprinkle cool water on each other!"

"Cool water" is Sawi idiom for "peace." Sprinkling cool water on each other could only mean "make peace." But did they really mean it?

According to my analysis of their cultural predicament, it should not be possible for them to achieve more than a mutual standoff through sheer physical separation of forces, unless one side was gullible enough to trust the other completely, which was unlikely in view of well-remembered Sawi history. So either they were shamming it, or else my analysis was about to be exploded. I hoped for the latter. But I could not imagine what proof of sincerity they could give to rule out the possibility of *tuwi asonai man.*

We hardly slept that night, wondering what daybreak would bring. Few of the Sawi slept either. Through most of the night we could hear their voices murmuring under the shrill carrier signals of myriad cicadas.

As dawn returned color and life to brooding longhouses, the jungle and the shimmering river, Carol and I were watching from our window. Tangy smoke from cooking fires drifted up through thatch roofs, roosters crowed, dogs yelped, pigs groveled for sago crumbs under the longhouses. But hardly a man, woman or child could be seen. Apart from the animal noises, it was deathly quiet, just as it had often been before a battle.

Then we saw Mahaen and his oldest wife climb down from their longhouse in Haenam and head toward Kamur. Now other people from Haenam—men, women and children—climbed down also and stood silently watching as Mahaen and his wife moved away from them. Mahaen was carrying a child, one of his own sons, on his back. His wife, Syado, was sobbing violently.

Carol and I moved tensely out onto our porch.

Now the people of Kamur were descending en masse from their longhouses also. Tension mounted as hundreds of eyes, including our own, followed the progress of Mahaen and his weeping wife. The trio was closer to us now, and Carol touched my arm apprehensively as we saw both the grim determination on Mahaen's face and the tears streaming from Syado's eyes. The child clinging to Mahaen's neck seemed passive and unaware of anything unusual.

The woman Syado looked over Mahaen's shoulder and saw the people of Kamur massed and waiting, staring at the three in anticipation. She began to shudder convulsively either from fear or deep sorrow, we were not sure which. Wiping the tears from her eyes, she suddenly wrenched the little boy from her husband's shoulders and bore him swiftly back toward Haenam, screaming as she ran.

Mahaen raced after her, trying to wrest the child from her arms, but Syado clung to the little boy with a strength born of desperation. Mahaen's oldest son, Giriman, ran forward from the crowd and intervened on his mother's behalf. With a roar of frustration Mahaen turned his back on them both and stalked back and forth in front of Haenam, shouting something unintelligible to us.

Clearly, Syado and Giriman had impeded his purpose, whatever it was. Now suddenly other women of Haenam were clutching their babies close to their breasts, crying out in apprehension. Men were running back and forth, gesturing, shouting. The village was in turmoil.

A loud shout from Kamur drew our attention. Something was happening in the center of the village. Leaving Carol on our porch, I ran to a better vantage point and watched intently. I saw a man named Sinau raise a little baby boy over his head for all to see. Then, his features contorted with unspeakable anguish, Sinau handed the child to his brother, Atae. "I can't bear to hand him over myself!" he cried. "Atae, you do it for me!"

Atae took the baby and strode purposefully toward

Haenam. But Sinau, the father, could not turn his eyes away from the helpless form of his baby son. The baby was like a powerful magnet drawing him.

Eyes brimming with tears, fingers writhing in despair, Sinau suddenly leaped toward the child, shouting, "I've changed my mind! I can't let him go!" Sinau snatched his little son out of Atae's arms. No one seemed to blame him. But neither did the uproar cease.

Strange, opposing forces of attraction and repulsion were building up an incredible tension between Haenam and Kamur. From my vantage point between the two villages, I could feel those forces crackling around me with an almost physical violence. The hair on the back of my neck began to crawl as I observed both villages in complete turmoil, as if travailing over some momentous plan that couldn't quite come to birth. Then out of the corner of my eye, I half-noticed a husky Kamur man named Kaiyo turn away from the crowd and climb up quickly into his longhouse.

Kaiyo's heart was pounding as he slipped away from his wife, Wumi, and ascended the stairpole into his home. Mahaen had failed! Sinau had failed! Both Mahaen and Sinau had many children, yet neither could bring himself to give even one.

Kaiyo had only one child, six-month-old Biakadon—lying there on the grass mat. Kaiyo approached the baby tensely, his heart wrenching within him at the thought of what he was about to do. Biakadon looked up at his father and smiled in recognition. He doubled his tiny brown fists and waved his arms in anticipation of being picked up.

"It's necessary," Kaiyo reminded himself. "There's no other way to stop the fighting. And if the fighting does not stop the Tuan will leave."

Kaiyo reached down and picked up Biakadon. Alone in the empty longhouse, he held the soft, warm, gurgling body of his son close to his chest one last time. He thought of the grief his deed would bring to Wumi, but there was no other way. Kaiyo looked toward the bright doorway at the far end of the longhouse, and began to walk toward it, his limbs trembling, his visage contorted by the conflicting emotions raging within him.

Biakadon's mother, Wumi, stood in the midst of the jostling, shouting crowd, absorbed in the common suspense of wondering whether there would be peace or not. Naturally if anyone would bring himself to the point of handing over a child, it would be someone who had many children and therefore would not miss one of them too badly. That was the reason it was out of the question for Wumi and Kaiyo to consider giving Biakadon.

"But," she wondered, "where is Kaiyo?" He had been standing right there beside her a few moments before. With a twinge of unease, Wumi's black eyes flashed toward the longhouse, just in time to see her husband leap down from the far end and begin running toward Haenam with Biakadon in his arms!

For a moment Wumi stood frozen with shock and disbelief, telling herself it was only a coincidence that

Kaiyo was heading that way with Biakadon. Then suddenly the knowledge that it was not a coincidence struck her with crushing weight. Wumi screamed and ran after Kaiyo, pleading with all the force of her soul.

But Kaiyo never looked back. His broad back kept growing smaller with distance as he raced ahead of her. Wumi felt her feet sinking in the mire of a small bog. In her anguish she had missed the trail.

There was no hope now. He was too far ahead. He had almost reached the waiting crowd among the Haenam longhouses. Even the hope that at the last second he would turn back of his own volition was gone.

With a piteous cry, Wumi let herself collapse into the slime in which she had become mired. Writhing uncontrollably, she kept repeating plaintively, "Biakadon! Biakadon, my son!"

I do not know a time when I have felt more intense sympathy for a fellow human being than I felt for Wumi at that moment. Glancing toward our home, I saw Carol holding Stephen tightly in her arms. I knew she was doing just what I was doing—feeling deeply Wumi's sorrow because of what our own son meant to us. Stephen looked up in amazement at the tears trickling down Carol's cheeks.

At the same time, two other emotions overwhelmed even our pity for Wumi. One was our concern for Biakadon. What fate awaited him?

Tearing myself away from the heart-rending spectacle of Wumi's sorrow, I followed Kaiyo toward Haenam. Thoughts of Canaanitic child sacrifices came to mind, and I decided if Biakadon's life was in danger I would use every power at my command to rescue him and return him safely to his mother.

The second emotion was intense curiosity. What were they doing? Why was it necessary?

The intensity of Wumi's sorrow belied my hope that Biakadon would soon be returned to her, implying that Kaiyo's action, whatever its purpose, was irreversible.

Kaiyo's chest was heaving with emotion as he reached the edge of Haenam. The leading men of the village were massed in front of him now, expectantly eyeing the child Kaiyo held in his hands. Kaiyo scanned the row of enemy faces before him. Maum, Kani, Mahaen, Nair—they were all there.

Then he saw the man he had chosen and called his name. "Mahor!" he cried.

Mahor leaped forward, his eyes bright with emotion. Kaiyo and Mahor drew near to each other. All the men, women and children of Haenam were crowding closer, their faces bright with anticipation. Behind him, Kaiyo could hear the roar of excitement from the people of his own village who were watching from a distance.

Kaiyo and Mahor stood face to face.

"Mahor!" Kaiyo challenged. "Will you plead the words of Kamur among your people?"

"Yes!" Mahor responded, "I will plead the words of Kamur among my people!"

"Then I give you my son and with him my name!" Kaiyo held forth little Biakadon, and Mahor received him gently into his arms.

Mahor shouted, *"Eehaa!* It is enough! I will surely plead for peace between us!"

Both villages thundered forth a series of *hahap kamans* until the very earth itself seemed to quiver with emotion. People now began calling Mahor by Kaiyo's name.

Suddenly Mahaen reappeared in the forefront of the crowd. Facing Kaiyo, Mahaen held aloft one of his other baby sons and cried, "Kaiyo! Will you plead the words of Haenam among your people?"

"Yes!" cried Kaiyo, holding out his hands toward Mahaen.

"Then I give you my son and with him my name!" As Kaiyo took the little boy, Mani, from Mahaen, a sudden cry of despair broke out from the back of the throng. Close relatives of the child had just realized what was happening.

Kaiyo was about to respond to Mahaen's gift when Mahaen urged him. "Go! Go quickly!" Kaiyo wheeled around and fled toward Kamur with his newly adopted son, Mani. Close relatives of the child tried in vain to overtake him.

As Kaiyo departed, Mahor shouted an invitation to the entire population of Haenam. *"Ini tim ke kanenai arkivi demake, ysyny asimdien!* Those who accept this child as a basis for peace, come and lay hands on him!"

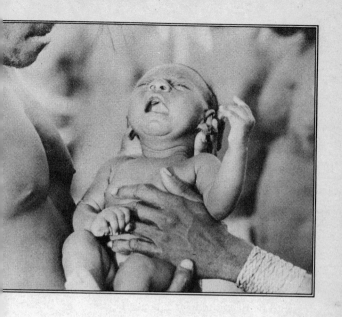

Young and old alike, male and female, filed eagerly past Mahor and laid their hands in turn upon tiny Biakadon, sealing their acceptance of peace with Kamur. The same ceremony took place in Kamur as soon as Kaiyo returned with Mahaen's baby in his hands. Kaiyo now began to go by the name of Mahaen.

Wumi meanwhile dragged herself out of the bog and staggered toward her home, weeping. A beautiful woman, she had now become a lonely, sorrowing specter, caked from head to foot in drying mud. Her cries were echoed by the moaning of those similarly bereaved in Haenam. Older women related to Wumi now came and wept with her in a vain attempt to assuage her grief.

Biakadon and Mani, meanwhile, were carried up into the manhouses in their respective adopted villages to be decorated for a peace celebration. It was the first time I could recall seeing so many Sawi men gathered together without a single weapon of war on their persons.

While the babies were being adorned, young men stuck feathers in their hair, brought out their drums, and began to dance. I managed to draw one of them aside. I had some questions to ask.

The young man's name was Ari. Exuberantly, he explained what had taken place. "Kaiyo has given his son to Haenam as a *tarop tim*, a peace child, and Mahaen in return has given a *tarop tim* to us!"

"Why is this necessary?" I asked.

"Tuan, you've been urging us to make peace—don't

you know it's impossible to have peace without a *peace child?*"

I must have seemed very ignorant as I shook my head.

Ari was astounded. "Do you mean," he queried, "that you Tuans are able to make peace without. . .?"

He paused a moment in deep thought, and then suddenly his face brightened with insight. "Oh!" he exclaimed. "I understand now. You Tuans never war with each other, so of course you don't need a peace child."

When Ari said that, a tiny bell started tinkling somewhere deep inside me. But it was very indistinct. I hardly paid any attention to it.

I was still reeling mentally under the shock of what I had witnessed. Still aching with pity for Kaiyo, Wumi, Biakadon, and the others. Still amazed at the fiery motivation and consummate strength of will which could move two such men to the superhuman subordination of parental instinct I had observed. Still electrified by the sudden vaporization of the atmosphere of war and hardly daring to believe the new beginning tingling in the air.

The voices of the young dancers rang out sharp and clear and joyful above the staccato roll of their drums. They made me aware that after six months of horror, shock and tension, I had virtually forgotten how to feel light and cheery. But was it right to feel light and cheery at Wumi's and Kaiyo's and Mahaen's expense? "Tuan, you don't understand . . ." they had warned.

If I had known my call for peace would provoke fathers to give up their sons, plunge mothers into grief, and cast babies into strangeness, what would I have chosen? To let the mothers continue suckling what their own wombs have borne, or to let violent men go ahead and kill each other? I had no answer.

But three hundred Sawi had laid hands on a peace child. And they were singing. And laughing. And inside me, the little bell was ringing a little louder.

"What will happen to Biakadon and Mani?" I asked. "Will they be harmed?" I was still on guard lest the joy these unpredictable people were expressing was only a deceptive prelude to human sacrifice. Or in case later, if someone violated the peace agreement, Biakadon and Mani might be slaughtered as hostages.

Ari hastened to reassure me. "They will not be harmed, Tuan," he said. "In fact, both our villages will guard the lives of these *tarop* children even more zealously than they protect their own offspring. For if Biakadon dies, Kamur will no longer be bound to a peace agreement with Haenam. And if Mani dies, Haenam will no longer be bound to a peace agreement with us."

I was both relieved and concerned. Relieved to know the two babies were in no danger of mistreatment. Concerned, because with infant mortality rates so high, the peace that had just been purchased at such high cost in human feeling could be lost before it had barely begun. An accidental fall into the river, a chance encounter with a death adder, or a sudden attack of cerebral malaria, and the awesome sacrifice would be rendered invalid, the parental agony ineffectual.

So, I mused—this peace depends upon the continuing life of the peace child involved. The little bell in my subconscious gave an extra loud ring that almost caught my attention.

The two babies were now fully adorned with tiny armbands and legbands of braided vine, to which golden tassles of twisted palm fibers were tied. Watiro, one of the leading women of Kamur, came forth from her village holding little Mani in her arms. She stood tall and erect on a knoll of high ground facing Haenam. Likewise, a leading woman of Haenam came forth with tiny Biakadon and faced Watiro at a distance of about fifty yards.

Suddenly the men and boys of Kamur surged past Watiro, beating their drums and singing. A corresponding throng erupted from the center of Haenam, advancing past their newly adopted peace child until they confronted their former enemies halfway between the two villages. They were all smiling at each other. Even relentless Ama now was smiling at Huyaham who had insulted him. Kaiyo's sacrifice was stronger than Ama's pride.

While the drums continued their steady throb, various individuals made their way forward from both groups and exchanged gifts such as axes, machetes, knives, shells, or necklaces of animal teeth. I learned that those who exchanged gifts also exchanged names.

Every man in Kamur obtained a Haenam name in addition to his own. Henceforth when someone from Haenam addressed him, they would call him by his *Haenam* name, indicating they no longer regarded him as a stranger, but accepted him as readily as they would accept the native son whose name he bore.

Conversely, people of Kamur would address citizens of Haenam by their *Kamur* names, accepting them as if they actually were the Kamur personages whose names they bore. To make the cross-identification easier, names were exchanged between persons of approximately equal stature and reputation.

Once the exchanging of gifts and the trading of names was completed, a strange dance ensued. First the men of Kamur assembled in a tight group while the men of Haenam whirled around them in a close circle. Then the men of Haenam spun off to one side and stood in another group while Kamur encircled them. At length the dance climaxed in a wild outburst of ecstatic shouting.

I named this the you-in-me-I-in-you dance. It symbolized the mutual peace-embrace of the two villages. The bell in the cellars of my mind was clanging louder now, impatient for me to recognize its message.

As Kamur and Haenam concluded the historic celebration by bearing their living, breathing peace tokens home in triumph, I called Narai and my other language informants to my office and sat down with them for a long, penetrating discussion.

The corrected picture was emerging. I had thought of the Sawi culture as based on a single pillar—a total idealization of violence, with its awesome manifestations of treachery, headhunting and cannibalism, aided when necessary by the inscrutable *waness* bind. In this view, peace could never be established, for the goodwill could have no credibility in the context of *tuwi asonai man* and the *waness* bind. Self-annihilation of the violence-honoring culture was prevented only by its fragmentation into small, mutually isolated communities.

The theory had seemed logical, watertight—yet somewhere in prehistory the ancestors of the Sawi had accomplished what the theory said could not be done. They had found a way to prove sincerity and establish peace even in the dread context of *tuwi asonai man* and the *waness* bind! Among the Sawi, every demonstration of friendship was suspect except one. *If a man would actually give his own son to his enemies, that man could be trusted!* That, and that alone, was a proof of goodwill no shadow of cynicism could discredit.

And everyone who laid his hand on the given son was bound not to work violence against those who gave him, nor to employ the waness bind for their destruction. The little bell clanged again, and this time it caught my attention. I perceived its message and gasped!

This was the key we had been praying for!

Part 3
A World Transformed

18

Stillness in the Manhouse

As I approached the Haenam-Yohwi manhouse, notes in hand, I stopped to watch some Sawi children at play. A few stood in dugout canoes and splashed each other by slapping their paddles on the surface of the Kronkel. Others were diving from the branches of a clump of *ahos* trees into the Tumdu, their slim, wet bodies glistening as they arced in the sun, their laughter rippling like the waves they created.

We had enjoyed two months of peace—the *tarop* was working!

Only once did we fear the peace might break down. A pig belonging to Kamur had been killed mysteriously not far from the village. The pig's owner suspected that someone from Haenam had been involved. Enraged, he and some of his friends took their weapons and started toward Haenam when suddenly Kaiyo intervened.

As the one who had received a peace child from

Haenam, Kaiyo possessed the acknowledged right to adjudicate all grievances between Haenam and Kamur. Approaching the potential treaty-breakers, Kaiyo had reached out and gripped their leader by his earlobes! I expected the fellow to react violently to this indignity, but instead he accepted it! He actually stopped in his tracks and lowered his bow, listening to Kaiyo's plea.

Meanwhile someone came running with Mani, the peace child adopted from Haenam, and held him in front of Kaiyo. Letting go of the man's earlobes, Kaiyo laid his hands on little Mani and said, *"Tarop tim titindakeden!* I plead the peace child!" Kaiyo continued, "If this child had died you would be free to do what you want to do. But he is not dead. He is still alive, and I am here as Haenam's *raendep hobhan,* 'advocate.' You may not fight against Haenam! My hand is strong!"

Whereupon Kaiyo returned his hands to the man's earlobes and began tugging at them. The man then turned and walked meekly back to his own house followed by his friends. If the aggrieved persons had remained hostile, Kaiyo would have severed their bowstrings, cut off the tips of any spears they might have tried to use, and thrown any other weapons in the river.

Once the aggrieved persons had returned to their homes, Kaiyo had thoroughly investigated the possibility that someone from Haenam had killed the pig. Finally both villages concluded the pig had been killed by a spy from one of several other communities bearing malice toward Kamur.

The crisis had been averted. The *tarop* custom had proved itself. The living peace child was indeed a culturally built-in antidote to the Sawi idealization of violence. The agony of Kaiyo, Mahaen and the two mothers had indeed purged all emotion of war from the two communities.

There were *two* pillars, not one, supporting the culture. Throughout their history, the Sawi had leaned first on one pillar and then on the other. Collectively, they were like a man standing on one leg until it gets tired, then shifting to the other leg.

For two months I had been scrutinizing every aspect of the second pillar, assimilating its abstract vocabulary, preparing a strategy. Now, as I climbed up into the Haenam-Yohwi manhouse, I felt again a wave of that bracing excitement which was more than just my own.

"You saw how horrified I was when Kaiyo gave you Biakadon," I said, snapping alternate fingers as the Sawi do at a point of tension. "When I saw Wumi writhing out her sorrow in the mud, I was almost ready to rush in among you, seize Biakadon, and give him back to his mother."

Mahaen, Mahor and others sat in silence, tracking my line of thought.

"I kept saying to myself, 'O that they could make peace without this painful giving of a son!' But you kept saying, 'There is no other way!'"

I leaned forward and placed my right hand palm down on the sago-frond floor. "You were right!"

Every eye in the manhouse was fixed upon me.

"When I stopped to think about it, I realized you and your ancestors are not the only ones who found that peace required a peace child. *Myao Kodon*, the Spirit whose message I bear, has declared the same thing—true peace can never come without a peace child! Never!"

Somehow the Sawi had forgotten the formality of repeating everything I said. It didn't seem necessary now. They had stopped thinking of me as a visitor in their manhouse.

"Because *Myao Kodon* wants men to find peace with Him and with each other, He decided to choose a once-for-all *tarop* child good enough and strong enough to establish peace, not just for a while, but forever! The problem was, whom should He choose? For among all human children, there was no son good enough or strong enough to be an eternal *tarop*."

I paused and searched their faces. Their curiosity level was rising.

"Whoever did He choose?" asked Mahaen, toasting a stick of beetle grubs over his cooking fire.

I answered with another question. "Did Kaiyo give another man's son, or his own?"

"He gave his own," they replied.

"Did you, Mahaen, give another man's son, or your own?"

"I gave my own," he replied, remembering the agony.

"So did God!" I exclaimed, following suddenly on Mahaen's reply and then looking sideways at the wall, a gesture meaning "think about that!"

248

I continued, "Like Kaiyo, God had only one Son to give, and like Kaiyo, He gave Him anyway! The child you gave, Mahaen, was no cast-off you wanted to get rid of—he was your *beloved* son. Biakadon too was a *beloved* son. But the Son God gave was even more beloved!"

Mahaen twitched his nose, a way of saying I understand.

"I have noticed how you respect words passed down from the ancestors. Hear now what ancestors of the Tuans say about the *tarop* Child from God."

I opened an English Bible and translated part of Isaiah's prophecy into Sawi: "Unto us a child is born, unto us a son is given: and the government shall be upon his shoulder: and his name shall be called Wonderful, Counsellor, The mighty God, The everlasting Father, The Prince—*Tarop*—of Peace. Of the increase of his government and peace there shall be no end."

And again from John's Gospel: "For God so loved the world that he gave his only begotten Son, that whosoever believeth in him should not perish, but have everlasting life!"[1]

The men leaned forward, gazing at the strange little "cluster of leaves" lying open in my hand, amazed at the message that had been trapped inside it and at my ability to spring that message out of it for them.

Mahaen looked at me and asked, "Is He the one you've been telling us about? *Yesus?*"

"He's the very one!" I replied.

"But you said a friend betrayed Him—if Yesus was

a *Tarop*, it was very wrong to betray Him. We have a name for that. We call it *tarop gaman*. It's the worst thing anyone could do!"

"You're right again," I said, looking Mahaen in the eye. "Despising the *Tarop* child of God *is* the worst thing anyone can do!"

I mused inwardly. Before this moment Judas had been a super-Sawi. Now he was a villain.

"Tell us more," Mahaen said, laying aside his stick of toasted beetle grubs.

A few hours later I was repeating the same message in the manhouse of Kamur.

"When you, Kaiyo, gave Biakadon, it was to sprinkle cool water on just *one* village—Haenam. Mahaen gave you Mani to make peace with just *one* village—your own. But Yesus is not a *Tarop* for one village only, but for *all* mankind—not only for Tuans, but for Asmat, Kayagar, Auyu, Atohwaem, and your-selves as well!

"When you, Kaiyo, gave Biakadon, you were very selective in choosing the individual to whom you would entrust your son's life. You chose the one you considered an ideal man—Mahor. But when *Myao Kodon* searched for a man worthy to receive His *Tarop*, He found no one! We were all unworthy of God's Peace Child. But did *Myao Kodon* say, 'I cannot give My Son because they are all unworthy'?"

Solemn faces studied me through wreaths of smoke from cooking fires, waiting for the rhetorical answer.

"No, He did not. He actually said, *'Kwai fidaema-kon!* I will give Him anyway!'"

I turned my attention again to Kaiyo. "Kaiyo, suppose someone had forewarned you that when you gave Biakadon, the people of Haenam would despise and even slay him—would you still have given him?"

"Certainly not!" he replied.

"But in the case of Yesus," I continued, *'Myao Kodon* knew beforehand that men would despise and even slay the Peace Child He sent to them."

A look of sheer awe crept over Kaiyo's face as he anticipated my next statement.

"But *Myao Kodon* loves us so much that. . . ."

There was stillness in the manhouse.

". . . He gave His Son freely even knowing men would despise and slay Him. In fact, through the wisdom of *Myao Kodon*, the men who shed the blood of Yesus actually provided a *raendep*, 'an atonement' to quench God's anger against men.

"They slew Him wickedly, but *Myao Kodon* was so *maraviap*, 'ingenious,' that even the very worst men could do only furthered His purpose! If it had not been so, there would be no hope for any of us."

I was about to narrate the victorious resurrection of the Peace Child when I was interrupted by an anguished keening from Hato. The look on the one-eyed patriarch's face startled me. Stark sorrow.

Hato's son, Amio, explained. "Not long before you came my father gave a peace child to the Kayagar. They took the baby and did not give one in return."

Amio winced as he continued, "Later we heard they killed the baby and ate it."

I drew in my breath sharply in horror. I reached out and touched Hato's hand and felt my being flow together with his in a mute sharing of anguish.

Near the edge of our cell of sorrow Amio's voice kept on explaining, "We learned then that Kayagar do not seal the peace by laying their hands on the living *tarop*, as we do, but by actually partaking of the *tarop* child's flesh. That way an accidental death of the child does not end the peace, because he is still living *inside everyone!*

"The people of Haenam and Yohwi chided us, saying, 'You Kamur people don't understand the Kayagar. You only understand the Auyu. If we had known you intended to give a *tarop* to the Kayagar, we would have warned you.'"

Someone else added, "That was the reason we almost started fighting with the Kayagar the day you arrived to build your home."

Stunned by this complex of revelations, I sat musing in silence, when Hato's voice came to me softly, "*Myao Kodon nohop kahane savos kysir nide?*"

My eyes welled at his words. He had said, "*Myao Kodon* must have been sad just like me."

The next day shadowy figures etched in smoke leaned forward to listen as I continued the same message in the somber manhouse of Seremeet village several miles downstream.

"In the case of a Sawi *tarop*," I reasoned, "you receive him bodily into your home, and he becomes dependent upon you for care and protection. But in

254

the case of God's *Tarop,* no one receives Him bodily."

"Then how can we receive Him?" asked an attentive listener named Morkay.

"You receive *Myao Kodon's* Peace Child by welcoming His Spirit into your hearts," I replied. "Then He becomes your Provider and Protector. And when the Spirit of Yesus dwells in your hearts, *Myao Kodon* will give you His *name* also. You will actually enter into a *hauwat,* 'name-exchange' relationship with the God of heaven and earth.

"He will link your names with the name of His Son and accept you for His sake. Then He will be in you, and you in Him, just as Kamur was in Haenam and Haenam in Kamur in their final peace dance!"

A murmur of discussion rustled along both sides of the long central corridor. As it gradually subsided, I rose to my feet to drive home the analogy as I had done in the manhouses of Haenam and Kamur. Every eye looked up at me expectantly as I towered beside a rack piled high with drying firewood.

"For moons without number your ancestors gave their children to establish peace—not knowing *Myao Kodon* has already provided one perfect Peace Child for all men—His own Son! And because your children were not strong, peace could never last. The children died, and you lapsed back into war again.

"That is the reason *Myao Kodon* sent me—to tell you about the Peace Child who is strong—the once-for-all *Tarop,* Yesus! From now on, let Sawi mothers keep their own babies close to their breasts—God has given *His* Son for you! Lay your hands upon Him

255

in faith and His Spirit will dwell in your hearts to keep you in the way of peace!"

I paused to renew my dependence upon the Holy Spirit before exclaiming, "If your *tarop* children, who were weak, could bring you peace, think how much greater will be the peace God's perfect *Tarop* will bring!"

Then I heard it again. The same soft, nasal expletive I had detected a day earlier at the end of my sessions with Haenam and Kamur. The Sawi call it *yukop kekedon yah motaken*. It signifies deep concern. I could hear its tiny explosions popping around me.

A man named Sieri expressed in words what his fellows were thinking:

"*Sin bohos!* It's true; our *tarop* children are not strong! I once knew a man who gave his son as a *tarop* to his enemies, waited a few days and then ventured a friendly visit to the village which had received his child. But as he approached the manhouse, men came storming out of it and threatened him with their spears.

"He exclaimed, 'Why do you threaten me? I gave you my son!'

"They replied, 'You gave us your son, but he died last night—what are you doing here?' Then they killed him!"

This recall touched off a still louder outpopping of *yukop kekedon yah motaken*. Men were rubbing their elbows as they sat on their grass mats, a sign that they were asking themselves, "What should we do?"

The look on their faces told me I had not only

discovered a parallel between their culture and the gospel, but I had also scraped a raw nerve as well—the obvious inadequacy of the Sawi peace child! And they winced collectively as I deliberately probed along that raw nerve.

They knew the peace-child concept was their *best*. Now they were finding what I too had found nine years before—*man's best is not enough!* They were approaching the realization that everyone's true self is waiting for him in the Son of God.

And if you don't find your true self *there*, you *lose* it! Forever!

I sat down again among them and began to talk about the change of behavior which follows reception of a peace child. I was tracing still another parallel between their culture and the gospel—the shared belief in repentance.

Once again, there was stillness in the manhouse.

FOOTNOTES

1. Scripture quotes are an English translation from the Sawi version of the Bible by Don Richardson.

19

Capsized Among Crocodiles

Throughout the months of March, April and May 1963, I continued accenting the Peace Child of God in the manhouses of a number of Sawi villages, gently inviting those who wanted to live by God's standard of peace to receive Him. Kani, Mahaen, Hato and others like them listened intently, even wistfully, yet every time they approached the threshhold of decision they drew back.

Fear of unfavorable reaction from the demon world was their main restraint. How would the spirits view this radical departure from ancestral tradition which the Tuan was proposing? If the demons reacted unfavorably—and the Sawi believed they most certainly would—could the Tuan and his God protect those who believed and their wives and children from disaster? The arguments for receiving God's Peace Child were reasonable and compelling, to be sure—almost everyone now understood why the Tuan and his wife had come—but what would the practical outworking be like?

For my part, I was wondering what else will it take to draw these men and their families to Jesus? I have presented Him in terms of a redemptive analogy from their own culture. I have used the key God provided, and in so doing have satisfied their intellectual need to understand the gospel. The basis for faith has been explained. Yet still something more is needed to precipitate their commitment to Him!

What other more compelling persuasion can I offer? Little did I realize what deeper forms of persuasion God still had in reserve for the Sawi, or what it would cost us to be the agents of that persuasion.

In May of 1963 the Dutch government ceded control of Netherlands New Guinea to the United Nations, with transfer to Indonesian sovereignty to follow in eight months' time. Not until a few years later would the Sawi and other tribes like them realize the staggering impact this political event would have on their future.

Basically, the policy of the Dutch government had been to establish a few widely scattered outposts, leaving intervening wilderness areas virtually untouched and uncontrolled. It was due to this policy of minimal development that tribes like the Sawi were left undisturbed even as late as the early 1960s. Only an occasional patrol officer, explorer, scientist, prospector or hunter ever probed the vast ungoverned areas, and when they did, they took little and changed little.

Indonesian control, however, would bring dramatic changes. Census takers would soon visit every village they could possibly reach. Police patrols would increasingly enforce civil law. Government-subsidized teachers would establish accredited schools in the Indonesian language. The harvesting of ironwood and other valuable timbers would begin in earnest. In some areas, crocodiles would be hunted almost to extinction for their highly prized skins.

Western oil and copper mining companies would abruptly construct massive bases in the pristine wilderness. Soon the chatter of cicadas and the mewling of birds-of-paradise would be drowned out in some areas by the roar of diesel generators, the clatter of helicopters and the thunder of dynamite hurling rock into the sky.

Even more significantly, opening the floodgates to heavy migration from teeming islands like Java, Sumatra and the Celebes would, within one generation, render the Sawi and their eight hundred thousand fellow New Guineans a minority people in their own land. These were only a few of the mammoth changes lurking over the jungle horizon in 1963—changes which would almost certainly plunge the Sawi and other unprepared tribes into severe cultural disorientation, apathy and even extinction, unless. . . .

Unless we, as the first agents of change to live among them, could effectively precondition them for survival in the modern world. For this, we must give them not only the Christian hope of eternal life, but also an ethic strong enough and resilient enough to sustain them through a one-generation riptide transition from the stone age to the twentieth century.

To be understood, that new ethic must somehow be tied in with their former culture. To assure their well-being it must also equip them to discern good and evil in strange new contexts, and then motivate them to choose the good! To endure, that ethic must spring from confidence in the unchanging love and justice of God.

I was convinced right down to the soles of my feet that the Bible I held in my hand was the God-ordained purveyor of that kind of an ethic. As such it was the key to well-being for the Sawi people in both this world and the next. But to become effective, it must win one essential commodity which all our prayer, persuasion and labor had still not brought forth—their response!

And time for the cultural preconditioning of the Sawi was running out.

Meanwhile, even as diplomats in New York, The Hague, and Jakarta were signing their embossed documents, headhunting and cannibalism persisted along the Kronkel River. A few months earlier, Asmat from the lower Kronkel had beheaded and devoured seven Sawi teen-agers from Mauro village. Later, in May 1963, the Asmat tried to forestall Sawi retaliation by sending gifts as a peace payment to Mauro. Mauro accepted the gifts and promised peace, but in actual fact they regarded the payment as in no way binding.

A few knives, dogtooth necklaces and other trinkets were not the same as a peace child. And they by no means balanced the loss of seven young men.

Thinking they had settled the matter, the Asmat became less wary. On May 20 a number of Asmat men, women and children were gathering shrimp along a mudbank of the Kronkel when suddenly the foliage above them swarmed with armed Sawi. Only one man escaped, paddling desperately downriver with a broken spear shaft protruding from his back. The heads of the others were soon mounted on bowtips and lined along the walls of the Mauro manhouse, gaping down at their own flesh sizzling in the fireplaces below.

Fearing massive Asmat retaliation, Mauro moved deeper into the sago swamps. So also did Seremeet who feared that the Asmat, failing to locate Mauro, would continue further upstream and pounce on Seremeet instead.

Haenam, Kamur and Yohwi likewise considered abandoning our riverside location out of fear of the Asmat, but decided they should stay to protect us! "With our three villages combined, we have enough men to withstand even a very large Asmat force," said Hato and Kigo.

Hato then added solemnly, "Tuan and Nyonya, we here have given up headhunting and cannibalism for your sake, but all around us. . . ." He swung his bow in an arc toward the horizon.

"I know," I replied. "I know also that if Carol and I should leave here, you would quickly revert to headhunting and cannibalism against your enemies.

because you have not asked the *Tarop* of God to give you new hearts."

Hato considered this for a moment. "*Sin bohos komai.* I think you're right!" he replied at length.

In June of the same year, Carol, Stephen and I returned to cool Karubaga in the central highlands to await the birth of our second child. On June 21 he arrived, attended by RBMU's Dr. Jack Leng. We named our baby Shannon Douglas.

On July 1 we returned to the Sawi with our delightful new baby, and with a guest as well! Winifred Frost, a colleague from Canada, had decided to spend a few days of her vacation with us so that she might witness the primitive beginnings of the work in a new tribe. By this time we had acquired an eighteen-horsepower outboard motor and a twenty-foot-long dugout which Hato, Maum and Kani, under close supervision, had fashioned with two features no Sawi dugout had ever known—a keel to improve its stability and a special mount for our outboard.

Late in the afternoon of July 4, we packed a lunch and set out with Winifred and our two babies for a restful boat trip upstream from Kamur, taking with us our Sawi houseboy, Mavo, to act as guide and helper. As we pulled away from the shore, I instructed Mavo to sit well forward in the bow of the three-foot-wide dugout to keep watch for any submerged logs which might lie across our course.

"Mavo, if you see any logs, wave to me," I said, increasing the speed of the boat to about twelve knots.

Mavo nodded, but as the squeal of the outboard grew louder and the boat leaped forward, I saw his eyes widen in fear. To him, it seemed we were flying at breakneck speed over the smooth, black surface. Twelve knots was about three times faster than Mavo had ever traveled on water. Apprehensively, he gripped the sides of the dugout. After a few minutes he'll get used to the speed and relax like Hadi and Er did on the *Ebenezer,* I reasoned.

Ten minutes later we were cruising around a jungle-walled bend nearly two miles upstream from Kamur when suddenly Mavo looked back and began signaling frantically for me to swing to one side. There must be a submerged log right in front of us, I thought, and reacted by swinging our craft just a little too sharply to the left. The dugout began to capsize. The keel I had been counting on for extra stability seemed to be no help at all.

I tried to regain our balance by swinging back to the right, but it was too late. Through one eternal second of horror I could see Carol clutching thirteen-day-old Shannon in her arms as she disappeared under the surface . . . Stephen falling into the black depths . . . Winifred and Mavo vainly leaning against the side of the dugout as it loomed up and over us all.

Then I hit the surface myself, still gripping the steering handle of the outboard. Dimly I could hear the muted roar of the engine throbbing under the surface; the whistle of the propeller spinning dangerously close to my shoulder. Then the motor died and we were drifting in silence in the very center of the crocodile-haunted Kronkel.

Winifred and Mavo surfaced almost at once and reached for the upturned keel of the dugout. Mavo, fearing crocodiles, pulled himself immediately on top of the dugout and sat benumbed on the keel. Carol, Stephen and Shannon were nowhere in sight.

"God help me!" I cried in a prayer of desperation—I've got to find them before the current separates us! And then a second thought exploded like a bullet through my brain—and before a crocodile finds them!

I knew there was little use searching visually under the water. It was impossible to see more than a couple of feet through the tea-dark discoloration of the Kronkel's algae. Instead I swam to the place where Carol had disappeared and groped in all directions under the surface, reaching with both arms and legs to try and make contact with her.

Suddenly Shannon's tiny face broke the surface right in front of me. Carol must have pushed him up so I could see him, I thought, as I quickly caught hold of Shannon and pushed him and his swath of dripping blankets up into Mavo's arms. Shannon broke forth immediately in a loud, startled cry. "Good!" I said to myself. "That means he hasn't breathed any water into his lungs."

Even as I whirled around to resume my search for Carol and Stephen, Carol surfaced. I caught her by the wrist and drew her close to the dugout, instructing her to hang on to the keel.

Now Stephen. Quickly I scanned the surface for some sign of at least a tiny hand reaching up.

I saw only reflections gleaming from the waves we

had created. And under the surface—only blackness.

Somewhere in that blackness my nineteen-month-old son was struggling, perhaps already sinking toward the bottomless ooze of the Kronkel's bed twenty feet below. Fighting back waves of despair, I reached out again with my arms and legs, trying to spread myself through as large a volume of water as possible. I could feel nothing.

"Perhaps he's trapped under the dugout! Father in heaven, keep the crocodiles away!"

Suddenly the thought flashed through my mind that Mavo from his vantage point on top of the dugout might be able to see down through the reflections better than I could, that is, if Stephen were still within two feet of the surface.

"Mavo, can you see Stephen?" I called in mounting anxiety.

My question seemed to jerk him out of his stupor. He scanned the water carefully. He pointed.

With a surge of hope I swam in that direction and then I saw what Mavo had seen—a tiny blur of blondness faintly visible through the Kronkel's murky water. A second later Stephen was in my arms. Surely by now he will have breathed in water, I thought. I was wrong. God in His mercy had given him sense not to try to breathe under water. As soon as I yanked him to the surface, he took a deep breath and began to cry. A moment later, Mavo had a baby under his other arm as well.

Now to get everyone ashore. Should we abandon the dugout and swim for it with the two babies? I noticed our plastic lunch bucket floating nearby—we could use that to bail the dugout, but it would take ten minutes at least! Surely the crocodiles wouldn't wait that long, nor would the fourteen-foot pythons which abound in the Kronkel.

The trouble was, if a crocodile intercepted one of us swimming to shore, we would have nothing to hold on to keep from being pulled under. Of course, if the croc was a large one even holding on to the dugout would be impossible.

If only someone were near with a canoe. Little chance, I thought—with only an hour of daylight left, no one will be lingering this far from the village.

"God help us!" I cried again from my heart. Then we heard it. Frantic paddling, as two-hundred yards away a black Sawi dugout darted out of the mouth of a small tributary. Gradually our unbelieving eyes registered two figures in the canoe—Mavo's own father, Taeri, and his younger sister, Aray.

"Taeri, hurry!" Mavo shouted above the cries of our babies. Old Taeri was nearly breaking his paddle as it was!

A minute later they were there beside us, braking their canoe to a halt with long, ironwood paddles and helping Carol up into their slim craft. As soon as Carol was seated in Taeri's canoe, Mavo handed her Stephen and Shannon.

Seeing how small Taeri's dugout was, Winifred decided to swim for shore rather than risk a second capsizing. Taeri paddled along beside her, ready to use the sharp upper tip of his paddle as a weapon against any crocodile which might choose that moment to attack.

Even as they headed for shore, Mavo and I turned our dugout upright and began to bail it out, using both our cupped hands and the plastic lunch bucket. I noticed that Mavo kept looking at me fearfully.

Paddling against the current, we reached home just before dark, shivering from the chill dampness of our clothes and from the thought of the utter tragedy which had nearly overtaken us. Sawi villagers lined the shore, anxious to enquire about what had happened. We touched land, and I began telling them about the accident. As I did so, I tried hard to make it clear that the whole thing was all my fault.

But no one would listen to me. Instead, the men on the shore turned angrily on poor Mavo, insulting and threatening him for being so careless with the Tuan and his family. Then I understood why Mavo had been so fearful following the accident. Since the overturning of a canoe usually meant the loss of valuable axes, machetes or knives, if not of human life as well, it was regarded as a serious "crime" among the Sawi and was usually followed by bitter recriminations and even the shedding of blood.

Mavo was in trouble and he knew it. Woebegone and afraid, he cowered in front of Hato and others as their indignation began to swell against him.

Suddenly Hato turned toward me with a length of heavy vine in his hand. "Tuan!" he said angrily, "Just say the word and I'll thrash him for you with this length of vine!"

I could see he fully expected my immediate compliance. But while Carol and Winifred took the children to our house, I walked past Hato and slid my arm around Mavo's trembling shoulders. Looking the old chief in the eye, I said evenly before them all, "None of you will raise a hand against my friend, Mavo. Without his help, I could easily have lost one of my children in the river. As long as I live, Mavo will be like a beloved son to me!"

The expression on Hato's craggy countenance underwent deep change. The other Sawi were listening in astonished silence as I continued, "Instead of blaming Mavo, join me in thanking *Myao Kodon* for saving us from tragedy!"

First Hato lowered his whipping vine; then he bowed his head. The others followed his example, listening as I poured out my gratitude to God in their tongue. When I opened my eyes, Mavo was looking up into my face, his own eyes brimming with tears.

Together we lifted the flooded outboard from the dugout and carried it to the house. It would take some work to get it going again.

The following Lord's Day I spoke to a large gathering of Sawi and Atohwaem on "Christ our Sinbearer." After the meeting, a tall young Atohwaem named Yodai approached me. Bilingual in the Sawi language, Yodai had been listening intently to the gospel for several months.

Often he had stood on our front porch for long hours, quietly observing as we ate our meals, worked, prayed, conversed with each other, and played with our children. He had occasionally helped us by entertaining Stephen or taking him for walks. He had been deeply moved by the near tragedy we had encountered on the river.

Facing me he said in his quiet, unaffected manner, "I am ready to trust in Jesus who came from God."

I took him aside and taught him to pray. I was glad when he started to pray in Sawi, because I wanted to listen in. After just a few sentences, however, he stopped and asked my permission to continue in his own mother tongue, so he could express his feelings more freely to God.

"Of course, Yodai," I responded.

Immediately a cool-sounding stream of Atohwaem flowed from him. It was completely unintelligible to me, but the glow in Yodai's eyes when he finished told me God had understood and accepted whatever he said. Reveling together in the presence of God, we headed home.

From a distance, Mavo stood watching, turning a stick over and over in his hands.

The joy on Yodai's face aroused a strange, new envy within him. Somehow, innately, he knew that joy was waiting for him also. He had even been dreaming about it. Now he wanted in, no matter what the consequences might be.

That same evening, after he had dried and put away the last dish from our evening meal, Mavo stood silently waiting until I noticed the longing in his eyes. A few minutes later, he too headed home with that joy throbbing through his being. A tiny crack had opened in the base of the first pillar.

The ascendancy of the second pillar had begun.

20

My Liver Trembles

Yodai and Mavo, however, were both very young men, and by no means leaders of their respective tribes. If the culture as a whole were to be transformed, the response of the patriarchs was essential. It happened in the Kamur manhouse a few weeks later.

I had just finished extolling once more the Peace Child of God and was gently inviting any who wanted God's standard of peace to receive Him when. . . .

"Tuan Don!"

I turned. Hato had risen and stood facing me squarely, his feet braced firmly on the sago-frond floor. His muscular arms were folded high in the manner of a headman. His chest heaved with emotion and tiny muscles flexed along his jaw. His single eye gleamed like a hot coal through the smoke and shadow of the manhouse.

From early childhood relatives and friends had instilled in him the Sawi fear of thinking, saying, attempting, eating or drinking anything that had not been sanctioned by the ancestors. To do so was to win the epithet *baidam,* "foolhardy." Some had called him *baidam* when, along with Kigo and Numu, he had chosen to stand and face the Dutch riverboats three years earlier.

But the decision he was about to announce now in the manhouse seemed to him far more daring. If they called him *baidam* when he chanced a merely *physical* encounter with the unknown, how much more so now.

Hato's voice was low and resolute. "Your words make my liver tremble (You have aroused longing within me)."

His voice choked with mingled dread and purpose as he continued, *"Myao Kodon fidasir Tarop Tim fasi fofadivi!"*

I had wondered how a Sawi headman would say it, and what it would feel like to hear it. Now I knew, for Hato had said, "I want to receive the Peace Child of God." And the sound of his words was saying *ga! ga!* to my ears!

I moved closer to him and laid my hand on his shoulder. His arms had fallen to his sides, and he seemed strangely oblivious to me and to the staring, wondering men seated around him. His one eye gazed past me, shining with a startling new radiance. There was no mistaking it. It was spiritual joy.

272

"Has He come in?" I whispered.

"*Ota, es!* He has come in!" he responded and then added, "*Yesus av!* It is Jesus!"

I turned from Hato and saw the eyes of every Sawi in the manhouse fixed upon him. I sensed there was no need to explain what had happened. They too could feel the benign Presence that had visited their headman. Some of them began to rub their elbows. Others were squirming uncomfortably.

From now on things would either get better or worse. But nothing could stay the same.

To the Hebrews He was the *Lamb of God,* to the Greeks, the *Logos.* But to the Sawi He was the *Tarop Tim Kodon,* the Perfect Peace Child—the ideal fulfillment of their own redemptive analogy! Ticking away like a time bomb through the ages, that redemptive analogy was now being detonated by the proclamation of the gospel. From now on, any Sawi who rejected Christ would see himself not as denying an alien concept, but rather as rejecting the Fulfiller of the best in his own culture!

I hurried home and found Carol radiant. I told her about Hato and she replied, "Hato's daughter, Kimi, prayed with me this morning. She said her father told her he wanted God's Peace Child, and she decided she did too!"

I gathered Carol into my arms and we thanked God together until we were interrupted by a little tug at knee level, and a soft voice calling in Sawi, "*Navo!* Daddy!" Stephen wanted in on our joy, so

273

I lifted him up and held him between us. The glow of health had long since returned to his cheeks.

"Honey," I whispered into Carol's golden hair, "This place has . . . it has. . . ." How could I express it? "It has the feel of the center of the will of God!"

"I know," she responded. "I feel it too!"

Within two weeks almost every member of Hato's household had shared in the patriarch's decision. Carol and I began teaching them almost daily whenever they were in the village.

One day I asked Hato, "What made you decide in favor of the *Tarop* of God?"

He replied, "When I saw that God's *Tarop* could give you peace even when your two sons had almost drowned, I knew everything you said about Him must be true. I decided He could take care of us too."

Hato's, Yodai's and Mavo's peers in all the surrounding villages were now watching them carefully, waiting in suspense to see if the reaction of the spirits might prove to be more than the three spiritual adventurers had counted on. For these other Sawi still higher levels of persuasion would be needed, and I trembled to think what it might take to provide that higher level of persuasion.

My trembling was justified.

21

The Living Dead

"Warahai is dead!"

The cry echoed like a thunder crack among the longhouses of Haenam that terrible day in January 1964. Startled men, women and children hurried out onto their porches just as the bearer of the tragic news beached his dugout in the shallows before the village. Pointing with his long paddle, he directed their still unbelieving eyes toward the *kidari*.

Three crowded dugouts were bearing rapidly closer. An ominous, quavering sound preceded them. It was the Sawi death wail. Sobbing broke out among the watchers in the village. As the three dugouts drew closer, some of the waiting men and women rushed down from their homes and threw themselves into the water, wailing frenetically.

We watched from our home as the three canoes arrived and Warahai's limp form was borne up into a longhouse on the shoulders of his friends. "Too bad they took him away to the jungle just as our treatments were beginning to do him some good!" I said to Carol as I headed toward the longhouse where Warahai lay.

If I had stayed home that day, it would have been so much easier. I could have shared in their sorrow from a distance and never known the truth. But something drew me up a trembling stairpole into that fateful longhouse and called me through a low doorway to stand among the writhing, naked forms of the male mourners. It kept me waiting where the air was so thick with the horror of death it could hardly be breathed, where every face was twisted with anguish for a human soul and wailing thundered in my ears like a sustained explosion.

I looked down through the interplay of shadowy arms and legs and saw the naked corpse stretched out on a grass mat. The dead man's mother, ancient Augum, crouched over the body of her son, covering his loins with her wizened face and hands. Her action was based on Sawi belief that a soul sometimes lingers in the generative organs even after other parts of the body are dead.

Other close relatives lay across the wasted legs and chest of the dead man, shouting his name, pinching his flesh or burning him with hot embers in a vain attempt to bring forth some movement reminiscent of life.

OF LIFE? I looked again. Yes, the dead man was breathing! Dread chilled my spine. The mourners must be faking it by pressing and releasing his rib cage, I thought. I struggled closer for an unimpeded view, but the sorrowers were now handling the body so violently I could no longer be sure of the apparent motion of breathing.

Slowly I reached for Warahai's wrist. With eerie suspense I pressed my finger where his pulse would have been. Immediately I felt a weak palpitation.

Dread gave way to excitement as I struggled to my feet. "I've got good news for you people!" I said, as I began waving my arms to catch their attention. "You think our friend is dead. Probably his breathing grew so weak you thought it had stopped; then in the anguish of mourning you failed to notice it has grown stronger again."

It took me several minutes to stem the cataract of wailing enough to be heard. I could hardly wait for the moment when my announcement would sweep despair from their faces and replace it with hope for the recovery of Warahai.

Finally Mavu took up my plea and bellowed, "Be quiet! Tuan wants to say something!" Only a low sobbing and moaning of the closest relatives remained. At last I could tell them!

"Warahai is not dead!" I proclaimed. "His pulse is still beating! If you look carefully, you will see he is still breathing!"

I thought they would rush forward to check Warahai's pulse and see for themselves that he was still breathing. No one rushed forward. No one even cast a glance at the now obvious rise and fall of Warahai's chest. They only stared at me with dull stares, as if impatient over this interruption to their weeping.

"Don't they understand?" I asked myself as I repeated the news and added, "You can stop wailing. Carol and I will give Warahai the best drugs we have. Perhaps he will recover."

Even as I was saying the words, the sick man's own wife, Anai, looked at Mavu in astonishment and asked, "Don't the Tuans know about death?"

Mavu's reply to Anai shocked me. "Naturally, since Tuans themselves never die, we can't expect a Tuan to understand death. We'll just have to be patient with him!"

So the Sawi thought we were immortal!

"You're wrong, Mavu," I protested. "We Tuans are subject to death just like you are. My father died when I was a boy. I understand about death."

Mavu and the others showed surprise. I had just exploded a myth. Then he rejoined, "Very well, you understand death as Tuans know it. But," Mavu looked sorrowfully at Warahai's faintly gasping, comatose figure, "obviously you don't understand Sawi death!"

"Why do you say that, Mavu?"

"Because you think Warahai is still alive."

"You yourself can see he is still breathing!"

Mavu smiled at me condescendingly. Then he continued, as if reciting a lesson to a child, "Warahai is still breathing because he is in a condition of 'apparent life' called *aumamay*. Sometimes in death a person's body keeps functioning for a while after his soul has departed. But it doesn't last long."

"How can you distinguish *aumamay* from temporary unconsciousness?" I countered.

Mavu smiled again. "The spirits tell us."

"How do they tell you?" I pressed.

Some of the mourners surrounding us were growing impatient. The matter under discussion was to them so elementary as to hardly bear repeating, and could not delay their weeping much longer. Renewed wailing began to well up around me.

"They tell us through a sorceress," Mavu explained matter-of-factly.

"And who is the sorceress who says Warahai is in *aumamay?*" I asked through the rising crescendo.

Mavu pointed with his chin toward the Haenam sorceress named Aham. I turned and looked at Aham. She glared back at me, as if sensing a challenge.

"Aham had a vision this morning. She actually saw Warahai's soul leave his body in *aumamay.*"

"She says she did," I countered, thinking fast. Mavu did not seem to understand the point of my remark. Aham was the most renowned sorceress in our community of three villages. It did not occur to the Sawi to doubt her word.

The mourners were beginning to handle Warahai violently again, burning him with hot embers and shouting in his ears. Under this kind of treatment, in his weakened condition, he would be dead before sundown. Sawi belief in *aumamay* would be still further confirmed! And Aham the sorceress would have precipitated the death of a patient we might have been able to save.

Before God I came to a decision. I raised my arms and shouted again for silence. Aham was watching me uneasily. When the din had subsided, I threw down the gauntlet.

279

"Aham has told you, in the name of the demons, that Warahai is already dead. In the name of Jesus, I tell you he is still alive! His soul is still in his body! Now I plead with you—stop wailing over him! Stop burning him with coals! Give us time to pray over him and treat him. If he recovers. . . ."

My heart was pounding violently. Warahai didn't look like a patient who might recover. His unconsciousness looked indeed like a terminal coma not unlike the Sawi concept of *aumamay.* I was laying everything on the line and the apparent odds were all in Aham's favor.

"If Warahai recovers, if he actually opens his eyes and talks to you and takes food—then you will know I have told you the truth in Jesus' name. But if . . ." (I was going to say 'if he dies,' and then I realized that wouldn't make sense to them because they considered him already dead.) ". . . if his pulse stops beating, you can believe Aham if you want to!"

Mavu laughed outright. "Warahai can't possibly recover!"

Someone else called, "Save your medicine for the living!"

Then hoary-haired old Boro rose to his feet. He was Warahai's eldest brother. He issued a gruff order to some of the younger men sitting nearby, "Go and build a gravehouse!"

The young men took their machetes and left in obedience to Boro. Then horror choked my throat as Boro looked at me and said, "We bury Warahai today!"

22

The Power of Aumamay

Burial among the Sawi means wrapping a corpse tightly in a grass mat, binding it firmly with vines around the neck, waist and ankles and then interring it in a small, coffin-sized gravehouse elevated five to fifteen feet above the ground. And since the Sawi were fully convinced that persons officially declared to be in *aumamay* were already dead, they had no compunction about interring them in gravehouses either.

I shuddered as I thought of the numberless unconscious men, women and children who, in past ages, had been interred in such gravehouses and deserted. Later perhaps, they regained consciousness, realized their plight and cried out in vain for help through the constricting, muffling mats bound tightly around their faces. Any passerby hearing their moans would not even stop to investigate—he would think it was only a case of *aumamay* lasting longer than usual.

Since the floor of a gravehouse was slanted to keep the body from sliding out, a weakened person, bound in the mats, would not even stand a good chance of wriggling out and falling to the ground to attract attention. Hence he could only sink back into a delirium of terror and die of hunger and thirst, if not from his original plight.

"Poor Warahai," I mused, looking down at his emaciated form. "You have fallen among thieves: the soul-stealing beliefs of your own people. And I don't feel free, like the priest or the Levite, to pass by you on the other side, just because your culture is different from mine. I am your keeper, Warahai!"

"Sorry, Boro," I said aloud. "It is *apsar* 'taboo' for me to let a man be buried while still breathing. You won't make me guilty of taboo by insisting, will you?"

Boro blinked and thought for a few moments. Then he turned and called the young gravehouse builders to return.

I looked around at the others and said, "Just to make sure you don't burn Warahai with hot embers and shout in his ears, I'm going to stay here the rest of the afternoon."

I went to the longhouse door and called Carol. Minutes later she arrived with medicine and gave Warahai an injection. Boro, Mavu, Augum and Aham looked at one another in perplexity, and then apparently decided simply to wait it out rather than venture a head-on clash of wills. They were sure Warahai would stop breathing before dark.

Four days and three nights later we were still struggling to save Warahai's life and still resisting the tide of public opinion which wanted to bury him as a dead man. Warahai had shown some signs of improvement, but not enough to shake Sawi belief in *aumamay* or in the infallibility of Aham's purported vision.

"Your medicine is making his *aumamay* last longer than usual, but it cannot bring back his soul!" was their conclusion. And now, just as darkness ended the fourth day, every sign of improvement in Warahai vanished and his condition deteriorated rapidly.

Our faith for the crisis was nearly exhausted. Our eyes were red from three nearly sleepless nights protecting the sick man from the mourners and trying to pray back the steady encroachment of death. Hato and other Sawi Christians were apprehensive lest I stretch the patience of Warahai's relatives too far.

Confused and weary, Carol and I sat down for our evening meal when suddenly a tumult of wailing erupted from the longhouse where Warahai lay. The same unspoken thought flashed between us— Warahai's pulse must have stopped!

Taking a kerosene lamp, I rushed through the night to the longhouse. It was packed with screaming, stamping, wailing people. Pressing through to the center of the crowd, I found them once again mauling and burning Warahai's limp body. Perhaps it no longer matters, I thought as I reached for Warahai's wrist.

"Lord God, have You abandoned us to defeat in this crisis?" I cried in silent anguish.

I gripped Warahai's wrist and searched for his pulse and hurled another mute petition heavenward.

"Are You going to throw away this opportunity to destroy a belief which over centuries has consigned thousands of helpless sufferers to premature death?"

I still couldn't find a pulse.

"If Warahai dies, belief in *aumamay* will be more deeply entrenched than ever, because Your servants challenged it and failed."

The whole longhouse was swaying. It was hard to keep my balance in the dim flickering shadows.

"You could heal him so easily! Don't You want the honor we are trying to win for You in the minds of these people?"

Despairing, I squeezed Warahai's wrist one last time.

"Why have I failed to find favor with You?"

His flesh pulsed against my fingertip weakly, but steadily. The battle was still on.

"Why have you suddenly started mourning like this again?" I asked.

Someone shouted at me, wild-eyed, "Aham had another vision! This time she saw a spirit ambush Warahai's soul and eat it! Now we know there is no chance you can make Warahai's soul return to his body! The spirits want us to bury him first thing in the morning!"

Through the shadows I saw Aham watching me, a look of triumph on her swarthy face. She had grown weary of having her infallibility questioned. She had

284

found a way to precipitate a final conclusion at once.

Resentful murmuring began to swell in the shadows around me. Warahai's aged mother pranced back and forth, scoffing at our intention to try to recover her son. Behind me and on all sides people began to say, "Go! Leave Warahai to us!"

Suddenly a sincere, understanding voice came out of the shadows. It was the voice of Narai, my language informant and one of the Christians. He said, "Tuan, you don't understand Sawi death. You'd better leave."

Other voices within my own being were already agreeing with him. The voices said, "You've done all that could be expected of you. If God wanted to give you victory in this, He'd have done it before now. Let the relatives take responsibility for their own actions.

"Warahai's eyes are already glazed. The death rattle is already in his throat. He'll die within twenty-four hours anyway. It's not worth creating a riot. It's only your pride that doesn't want to accept defeat. Give up!"

But then I tried to imagine myself consenting next morning when they wrapped the woven grass shrouds around Warahai's still breathing face and pulled the vines tight. I tried to picture myself working up courage to contest their belief in *aumamay* on some later occasion, after having failed in this one. No, that cannot be.

I tried to summon courage, the same courage God had given me for past crises, but it was gone, already disintegrating inside a cocoon of despair. I pressed my spirit naked against God, that He might conceive new courage within me. He conceived it and it grew, actually feeding on the despair that killed its predecessor. In a few moments it was ready to be born in action.

"Lord, what shall I do?"

"Get Warahai out of here!"

"But Lord, for that I'll need help. Who among these people will help me? I'm alone."

"Look around you!"

I started to look around and immediately Mahaen's lean, somber face stood out in the light of my lamp.

"Mahaen, come here."

He came as if he had no choice.

I spoke softly in his ear. "When I lift Warahai onto your back, carry him out of here and over to my storehouse. I'll clear the way ahead of you."

Mahaen searched my face. How could he possibly comply? Over the past months he had grown increasingly friendly toward me, though on this occasion he was barely convinced of the wisdom of my decisions.

"Warahai is still alive! Help me prove it!" I urged.

Mahaen's features firmed with decision. "*Fisahaemakon!* I'll carry him!" he said.

I set down the lamp and lifted the unconscious invalid up onto Mahaen's back. He staggered to his feet under Warahai's weight. Anger flared around us as we headed for the doorway.

Warahai's younger brother Kimi stood ready to oppose us with his weapons. Mahaen hesitated.

"Keep going!" I urged.

"Tuan, Warahai's dead!" Mahaen cried, weakening under the pressure of the crowd.

"He's not dead! Keep going!"

Suddenly another youth named Aidon stepped out of the mass of protesting people. "I'll help you carry him!" Aidon said firmly, lifting Warahai's legs onto his shoulders.

Encouraged, Mahaen moved out through the doorway and down the notched stairpole, followed by Aidon.

I was keeping an eye on Kimi and the others. They had not prepared themselves for such an unexpected stratagem. Taken by surprise, they followed us through the darkness, shouting, "Bring Warahai back! Bring him back!"

We kept going until we were inside the storehouse. I closed the door against the crowd. Augum, Warahai's mother, leaped back and forth outside our door, crying bitterly, while Kimi shouted, "Tuan, let me carry him back to the longhouse!"

As firmly as possible I answered, "No!"

Soon the crowd dispersed to their homes. For two hours their cries of anger grew louder until I wondered if they were working themselves up to storm the little building. They could have done it easily.

Toward midnight, the village grew quiet. Aidon returned home, while Mahaen remained to watch with me over Warahai's motionless form. About midnight, Carol joined me in the storehouse. Mahaen sat listening quietly as we prayed again for Warahai's recovery, and sang a hymn of praise to God.

As dawn broke, I awoke to hear an ominous rattling in Warahai's chest. Pneumonia was causing his lungs to fill with fluid. To prevent suffocation, I used my battery hydrometer to suction as much of the fluid as possible from his throat.

Later in the day Carol pointed to our remaining box of penicillin ampules and said, "This one man is rapidly depleting our supply, and it isn't doing him any good. Should I continue?"

"No," I replied. "If our drugs could help him, surely we would have seen an improvement by now. Other patients will need those drugs. From now on it's prayer and prayer alone."

We looked down at Warahai, His breathing was growing steadily fainter. His skin hung like loose parchment over his almost fleshless skeleton. His half-open, unblinking eyes seemed already to be gazing into the next world.

Carol reminisced, "In the hospital where I trained as a nurse, patients like Warahai were kept under constant intravenous feeding, and we had electrical equipment to extract fluid from their lungs. Even so, some of them died, and they were not as far gone as Warahai.

"I'm sure there isn't a doctor in the world who would say there was any hope for him apart from. . . ."

". . . a miracle?" I responded. "That's all we can hope for now."

Later that day Mavo appeared suddenly in the doorway of our home. "Tuan," he whispered, "Kimi and others of Warahai's relatives are coming. Kimi is hiding a bone dagger behind his back. Be careful."

I thanked Mavo and looked out through our screen window at the approaching party. Their eyes were full of hurt and blame. They seemed to say, "Why are you making us drag this thing on day after day? But for you, Warahai would have been buried long ago. You are simply making it more painful for all of us."

"Kimi!" I called suddenly, "You are hiding a bone dagger behind your back—remove it from my yard at once!" Startled, Kimi handed the weapon to a boy standing near him who promptly carried the weapon back to the village.

At sunset, Kimi, Boro and other relatives of Warahai returned in a much more conciliatory mood. "Tuan, we still believe Warahai is dead and should be buried, but we have decided to respect your wishes. Let us take him back to the longhouse, and we give you our word that we will not mourn over him, burn him with embers or try to bury him as long as his pulse is beating. When his pulse stops, we will call you so you can see for yourself that it has stopped. Only then will we bury him."

My heart warmed toward them. At least this small measure of victory had been won, though I still hoped for much more. I gave them permission to carry Warahai back to the longhouse. His coma was deeper than ever.

As darkness fell, Warahai's relatives were true to their word. No sound of wailing or commotion could be heard from Haenam village. Five days of struggle, and how would it end? How much longer could Warahai continue breathing while God waited?

In agony of spirit, I reached for our book of topical Scripture readings, turned to the evening reading for January 30, and began to read aloud, "O Thou that hearest prayer. . . . The eyes of the Lord are upon the righteous and His ears are open unto their cry. . . . When he cries unto Me, I will hear, for I am gracious. . . . He will fulfill the desire of them that fear Him. . . . O Lord, Thou art our God; let not man prevail against Thee. . . . If two of you shall agree on earth as touching anything that they shall ask, it shall be done for them of My Father which is in heaven."

The two of us sat and looked at each other in the soft lamplight. If it had been only one isolated promise in the middle of a passage, it would have been sweet enough. Instead unexpectedly, promises heaped upon promises had leaped forth from one page, each vying with the others to see which could encourage us the most.

We smiled at each other, misty-eyed and weary, yet suddenly overflowing with joy. An audible voice could not have made the message clearer. God had heard our prayer.

In the morning Haenam was strangely quiet. I walked slowly toward the village. Yamasi, one of Warahai's brothers, stood waiting beside the trail. He pretended not to notice the question in my eyes as he whittled on a stick. So I voiced it, "How is he?"

Yamasi glanced sheepishly toward me and said, "He's been talking to us."

"He's been talking?"

"Yes."

My heart was turning cartwheels inside me. "What did he say?"

"He said to his mother, 'O Mother, don't be sad!'"

Like a man in a dream, I walked past Yamasi and climbed up into the longhouse. Warahai opened his eyes and looked at me as I bent over him. His breathing was free and normal.

"Konahari, Warahai!" I said to him.

"Konahari!" he replied, smiling.

He was leaning back across his mother's lap. His wife and children and other relatives were gathered close around him. I lifted his wrist in my hand. The chill of near-death was gone. His pulse was stronger.

The normally noisy longhouse was still as a cathedral. I looked around from face to face. One by one, Warahai's relatives dropped their gazes toward the floor.

"Do dead men say *konahari?"* I asked quietly.

After an embarrassed silence, someone said, "No. Dead men never say *konahari."*

"And if Warahai's soul had been cut up and eaten by a demon, would he be looking around at us as you now observe?" I continued.

"We listened to a lie," said Mahaen solemnly.

I looked around for Aham, but she was nowhere in sight.

"We nearly buried a living man," said Boro, staring at the wall.

"How good is the kindness of Jesus!" said old Augum, stroking Warahai's forehead.

I hurried home to tell Carol and we returned together with nourishment for Warahai. He had been several days without food. After he had eaten, we praised God openly for Warahai's recovery and then hurried to Kamur to share our joy with the Christians there.

On the following day, four of Haenam's leading men received Christ. One of the four was Aham's husband. Another was Mahaen. Still another was Kani, Haenam's "master of treachery."

Later, in the Seremeet manhouse, Morkay rose to his feet. There was a new light on his usually soulful countenance as he said, *"Myao Kodon* has shown us His hand is strong! As for me, I believe!"

Sieri and his son Badan followed Morkay's example, as half of Seremeet village would follow before two more years had passed.

When I returned from Seremeet I visited Warahai again in his longhouse and found him sitting unaided by his fireplace. He greeted me cheerfully. I sat down and talked with him and then prayed with him before leaving the longhouse. As far as I could tell, he too had come to a genuine trust in Christ.

I was disappointed to find that Warahai's clan was making no effort to obtain fresh food for him from the jungle, and he was finding the stale sago they offered him very unappetizing. I urged them to make better provision for him, but with little effect. As an example, Carol and I sent occasional gifts of fresh food to Warahai.

Within a few days Boro, Aham, Kimi, Yamasi and others of Warahai's relatives made it clear that they had decided to reject Christ in spite of God's mercy in the healing of Warahai.

"You are indeed free to reject God's Son if that is your choice. But remember this," I counseled, "You now possess insight none of your ancestors ever possessed, and God will judge you according to that insight. The same God who shows kindness can also punish."

Boro replied, "Let those believe who want to believe. We'll stay as we are."

Without another word, I turned and left him. Outside Boro's longhouse a group of Haenam believers stood waiting. We walked together toward a small meetinghouse that now stood on a nearby knoll of high ground.

Others who had recently trusted came down out of their longhouses and joined our jubilant conversation as we proceeded. There was my friend Mahaen and lovely Waiv, old Wario's daughter, soon to be given in marriage to Mahaen.

With them came young Amus and his bride-to-be, Aiyau, accompanied by thoughtful Kani, who had carried so many dark memories so long. Yodai, Hadi and a handful of other Atohwaem believers from Yohwi followed them, along with a band of laughing children who still didn't understand what it was all about, yet were drawn spontaneously to share in our joy.

Inside the meetinghouse, the Kamur believers were waiting: Hato, his wives, his sons and his daughters; Kaiyo, who had given the peace child and opened my eyes. Mavo, the quiet helper, and winsome Isai, the boy who had climbed a tree to watch the two riverboats surge past his village, were also there.

Beside them were Isai's father, Mairah, whom Isai had brought to Jesus, and Seg, who had secretly observed me standing in the leafy arena when I chose the site for my home. Amhwi the sincere, who had learned to trust by watching Mavo, completed the group.

Carol handed me a cardboard box. A hush fell as I began to open it.

"We have a surprise for you."

I lifted a handful of newly stenciled white booklets out of the box. Then, assuming an air of deepest confidentiality, I whispered audibly, "We're going to teach all of you to read!"

Eager hands of young and old alike reached up as I handed out copies of the first Sawi primer. The initial lesson was how to hold the primers right side up. The second lesson was how to open one page at a time. Hato grinned avidly. He was learning fast.

It was a pleasant interlude before our next shock.

23

Eyes Red with Watching

The flimsy poles of the gravehouse trembled under the frenzied assault of the mourners. Some leaned against its sides, moaning in abject grief, their arms upstretched toward the corpse above them, their fingers writhing as if trying to grip some intangible substance of the departed soul. Others mounted the platform itself and hovered vulturelike above the dead body, shrieking like banshees.

The mourners' bodies were caked in mud. The air was thick with the stench of the corpse, but they willingly endured it. Death-flies swarmed around their faces, but they paid no attention.

Through nine hot days and nine humid nights they had waited while that stench grew stronger and the fly swarms thicker. On mats in the lone jungle long-house nearby, they had sat waiting, breathing it in.

To do so was only the first stage of a Sawi veneration procedure called *gefam ason*. Now the relatives were keyed to carry out the remaining progressions of *gefam ason,* ready to consummate their grief in the time-honored manner.

Suddenly a young relative worked his way between two of the supporting poles under the gravehouse. He danced feverishly, calling aloud the name of the departed one. And as he danced, maggots and rotting flesh, shaken loose from the trembling platform above him, rained down upon his shoulders, his forehead, his hair. The second level of despair had been enacted.

The pitch of wailing rose higher in sympathy with the young man's extreme devotion. Presently the young man stepped out from under the gravehouse and staggered toward the still pools of a nearby stream. Now that his ordeal was over, and he dared to relax his will, he began to heave convulsively as waves of nausea overcame him. Moaning and retching with mingled sorrow and revulsion, he let himself sink down into the cleansing water.

All eyes now turned to the men who surrounded the corpse on top of the burial platform. It was up to one of them, if the next level were to be attained. Perhaps they would fail.

Staring intently at the seething horror between them, the men in question knelt in a tight circle. Their hands trembled. Their bodies went rigid.

Suddenly one man raised his arm high above the corpse and with a shrill apocalyptic screech drove his clenched fist deep into the putrid body cavity. For a few brief seconds the man's face registered a shock of unutterable ghastliness, gouging an eternal memory in the minds of all who beheld him. Then, swooning from severe emotional exhaustion, he sagged slowly over the side of the platform, dragging his dripping hand after him. The third level had been achieved.

The other mourners caught him and carried him up into the longhouse and set him down on a grass mat, where he waited until freshly cooked sago was brought to him. Taking the sago in his contaminated right hand, he raised it to his lips and ate it, while the other mourners wailed around him with unbelievable intensity. The fourth and ultimate level of despair had been expressed.

The pinnacle of highest emotion had passed. Most of the mourners drifted slowly up into the longhouse, as golden evening burned across the eden of towering sago palms that surrounded their clearing.

A handful remained to weep around the gravehouse: Boro, Augum, Yamasi and Kimi. As they wept they called aloud the name of the freshly wounded corpse above them: Warahai.

Red shafts of sunset pierced the shadows around me. Why did God let him die? For ten days he had gained strength, venturing out of his home, even sitting up late at night to talk with his friends. Then without warning on the eleventh day, Warahai lapsed into unconsciousness. And on the thirteenth day, he died.

Was it only lack of fresh food that killed him? How

I wished we had sent him more of our limited supply of fruit and eggs! Or were the Sawi Christians right in concluding that God had chosen to fulfill my warning to Boro, thus confronting unbelievers with a still higher level of persuasion?

For nine days I had been asking questions such as these. I had hoped Warahai would remain as a living evidence of God's mercy and power. But God had claimed the evidence for Himself.

Still, I had my consolations. Sawi belief in *aumamay* had been shattered wherever the news of Warahai's recovery spread. The faith of the believers had increased, and many new believers had joined our company.

I drew a deep breath and headed for home just as a lone figure beached his dugout in front of our house. He greeted me as I reached our front steps.

"*Konahari!*" I replied. "Where have you come from?"

"From Boro's longhouse on the Sagudar tributary," he replied. "They had a ceremony for Warahai today. Warahai was a distant relative of mine so I thought I should attend."

"What ceremony?" I asked. "I thought Warahai was interred nine days ago."

"He was," the man replied. "Tuan, haven't you heard about *gefam ason?* It means 'touching the stench.'"

"No. What is *gefam ason?*"

The man thrust his paddle blade into the ground and looked at me as if ready to speak. Then he thought better of it, made some excuse for having to leave, took his paddle again and started to walk past me.

I laid my hand on his arm. "You better tell me," I said.

"I'm not sure you would approve, Tuan."

"I'll find out later anyway."

He knew that was true. Leaning on his paddle, he began to divulge the ancient horror he had witnessed that very day.

That night Carol and I lay awake, troubled by this newest revelation of the Sawi mind. So this was another of the things Boro had chosen in preference to Christ!

How could such a custom ever have found acceptance in the first place? What awesome sense of tragedy had first spawned it? And how strong, how deep, must the dark compulsion be that made successive generations willingly perpetuate a custom repulsive even to themselves!

Stung by the seeming impossibility of ever comprehending the soul of such an enigma, I groaned aloud into my pillow. What should I do about it? How could I tackle what I could not understand?

I knew it would not be enough simply to tell them: "Look here! Stop doing this! It's not nice!" They already knew it wasn't nice. Obviously the very unniceness of it was somehow related to its purpose, like the deliberate unniceness of the debt-incurring deed in the *waness* bind.

Then my breath stopped in my throat. Could that be it? I sat upright in bed, wondering.

Could the custom called *gefam ason* simply be a way of trying to impose a massive *waness* bind on . . . on not just an invididual, but on the whole supernatural world? The idea was forming.

But what could be the purpose of such a large-scale *waness* bind, carried out by unnumbered Sawi over aeons of time? Could it be to coerce an eventual abrogation of death itself? I was determined to check out this hunch. Morning couldn't come fast enough.

Slowly I waded along the flooded corridor between twin rows of Haenam and Yohwi longhouses. The high wailing sound of a Sawi dirge grew louder as I drew close to its source. Sitting enwreathed in smoke beside her fireplace, an old, toothless woman was rocking back and forth as she mourned the death of Warahai.

The words of her dirge were mostly unintelligible to me, as her voice was broken with sobbing. I tried in vain to comprehend the message. Then I saw Mahaen. He had come down the stairpole of his home to meet me.

"Mahaen, tell me what that woman is saying."

He replied, "She is saying,

" 'Words of *remon!* Words of *remon!* Why are you delaying so long? Because of your delay, death has taken my son away!

" 'Words of *remon!* Words of *remon!* Our eyes are getting red watching for your coming!

" 'Words of *remon!* Words of *remon!* Will you come from upstream? Will you come from downstream?

" 'Words of *remon!* Words of *remon!* Hurry, or death will take us all away, and no one will be left to welcome you.' "

The poignancy of this Sawi poem, set in the grim context of the sorrowing village, and with the accompaniment of the old woman's wailing, was overwhelming. In a voice hushed yet eager I asked, "Mahaen! What is *remon?*"

We began to wade toward my thatch-roofed office as Mahaen explained. *"Remon* is what happens when a caterpillar escapes death by transforming into a moth, bursting out of its cocoon to live on in a new body. It also describes the way a lizard or a snake escapes death by shedding its old skin."

Remon, then, was approximately equivalent to our English word "regeneration."

"And what are the *words of remon?*" I questioned.

"It is said that long ago men also possessed the power to *remon* their bodies and keep on living endlessly. Then a lizard and a *karasu* bird had an argument. The lizard, as the symbol of *remon,* said men should remain free from the power of death. The bird, because it dies so easily, was the symbol of death. He insisted that men should become subject to death like himself, and even started cutting poles for the first gravehouse!"

"What happened?"

302

"The snake kept saying *'rimi! rimi!* renew! renew!'* These were the words of *remon.* But the bird kept saying, *'sanay! sanay!* decay! decay!'* The argument went on and on until finally the lizard gave in to the will of the bird. From that time on, men began to die."

"Why did the lizard give in?"

"We don't know. Something must have happened, but we've forgotten what it was."

"Is that the end?"

"No. Our ancestors said that someday the words of *remon* will come back to us. After that, those still alive will renew their bodies like the lizard and the caterpillar. There will be no more death."

My whole being thrilled as the utter significance of Mahaen's words bore in upon me. Then I remembered to ask, "And what does the custom of *gefam ason* have to do with all this?"

Mahaen stopped in his tracks and glanced at me quickly. "You know about *gefam ason?*" he asked.

"I know what men must do to fulfill its requirements. What I don't know is why it is necessary."

"We do it because our ancestors did it," he offered flippantly.

It was a favorite Sawi catch-all answer for a thousand difficult questions. I brushed it aside. "You can try an answer like that on your little children, but don't try it on me," I said smiling.

Mahaen laughed. "Really, Tuan, I'm not sure I know any other. . . ." His voice trailed off. He was thinking. He thought for a long time, as I waited ankle deep in the mud, my pen poised over my notebook.

"Perhaps it is . . . ," he began at last, and I wrote down the Sawi as it flowed from him, ". . . *rigav bohos savos keroho farakotai remon sin fatar ni naha saren gani!* . . . so that when mankind has reached the fullest measure of sorrow, the words of *remon* may come the more quickly!"

I thanked Mahaen and decided to question my other language informants. Some of them would venture no opinion on the significance of *gefam ason.* Others offered opinions similar to Mahaen's. Still others who had no opinion of their own immediately accepted Mahaen's opinion when it was suggested to them.

I had found some indication, at least, that the *waness* bind and *gefam ason* both spring from the same root—the belief that ends not attainable by force or ordinary persuasion can be won by subjecting one's self to extreme humiliation or mortification. In other cultures the same psychological bent may be expressed in such ways as accident proneness, penance, protest fasting, flagellation or self-immolation.

But the New Testament has a single, clear answer for prisoners of this nearly universal complex of compulsions—the humiliation and death of Christ on our behalf! His death alone could impose a *waness* bind upon the laws arrayed against guilty men. His resurrection offers the only hope of *remon* we can ever know! Thus my strategy for dealing with the morbid, almost psychopathic Sawi obsession with the corpses of the dead was emerging.

Sooner or later the Indonesian government would outlaw *gefam ason* for sanitary reasons alone, but this would not remedy the underlying spiritual deficiency which had given birth to the custom in the first place. Sawi culture had struggled through the millenniums without an adequate answer to the despair imposed on man by death. The Christian doctrine of the Resurrection was the God-given antidote to that despair, and Sawi belief in the future return of the words of *remon* was the redemptive analogy through which that antidote could enter.

I summoned the Christians of Haenam, Yohwi and Kamur to a meeting. Hato, Kaiyo, Mahaen and the others listened attentively as I summarized my argument. I began with Jesus' raising of His dead friend, Lazarus, and described His own resurrection on the third day after death.

Now I concluded, "He raised others from death. He rose from the dead Himself! He proclaimed Himself to be the Resurrection and the Life in Person!

"His words are the words of *remon!* And they have already reached you! They bring you first the *remon* of your inner man through the Holy Spirit dwelling within you, to be followed, according to the promise of Scripture, by the *remon* of your bodies on the Day of Christ!

"You have long said your eyes are red with watching for the promise of *remon*—I hope they are not too red to recognize it now that it is here! And if you believe Jesus' words are the true words of *remon*, do you still need to practice *gefam ason* on the dead bodies of your loved ones?"

305

Hato rose immediately to his feet. "Thank God you told us that! Now we can quit that ugly practice!" he exclaimed.

Then he turned to his own relatives and gave them stern instructions, "When it comes my turn to die, let my body rot in peace. If you carry out *gefam ason*, it will mean you really don't believe the promise of *remon* in Jesus." His relatives nodded in agreement.

One by one, the other believers stood up and made the same request of their friends that Hato had made. Now, for the Christians at least, the Indonesian government would not need to suppress *gefam ason* among the Sawi, for the gospel was already supplanting it. Even as the believers were still speaking, I stood hushed and amazed before God.

"I thank You, my Father, for laying the groundwork for our ministry to these people. The Sawi were strangers to our Judeo-Christian heritage, yet You so providentially ordained these redemptive analogies within their culture ages ago, so that one day we would find and use them for Your glory. You were concerned, not only to send messengers, but also to prepare a culture to receive their message.

"As You prepared the Hebrews and the Greeks, so also the Sawi were not too insignificant or too pagan to receive this much of Your providence.

"And yet Your Word, not their analogies, is the standard. I see now more than ever why You are called the God of wisdom and the God of love and the God of power.

"I praise You!"

24

Out of the Ancestral Cocoon

Circling twice, the Cessna wheelplane swooped down into a tree-walled canyon newly carved through nearly a mile of southwest New Guinea jungle. In clearing for the airstrip, hundreds of trees had been felled by Sawi axemen, providing timber for improved Sawi dwellings and firewood for several of their villages.

Swamp water sparkled under the lowering wings until the aircraft touched down on a sixteen-hundred-foot strip of raised soil waiting at one end of the clearing. Under our supervision, the Sawi had excavated thirty-five hundred cubic yards of clay by hand and carried it on rice-sack stretchers to raise the airstrip above the surrounding flooded swamp.

The entire project had taken four months, providing abundant payment in steel axes, machetes, knives, soap, salt, fishline, fishhooks, mirrors and, for those who requested it, clothing. Nearly two hundred Sawi men had found in the project an exciting new outlet for energies once devoted to war and headhunting.

At the far end of the airstrip, a 110-foot ironwood bridge arched across the Tumdu, connecting the airstrip with our home. People from Haenam and Kamur streamed across it to welcome the aircraft. Stephen and Shannon were among them, followed by Carol carrying our third son, Paul. The village of Yohwi was not present, having long since returned to its upstream haunts after a serious quarrel with Haenam.

Beyond the bridge stood the three-bedroom dwelling I had built five years earlier to replace our original thatchbox. Here also several hundred cubic yards of clay had been built up and lawned into a yard supporting a parklike grove of young coconut palms, breadfruit, guava and lemon trees. The whole was bordered with hedges of pineapple and spangled with beds of canna lilies, hibiscus, bougainvillea, and frangipani. These were only a few of the fruits and flowers we had introduced to the Sawi.

Beyond our yard stood the medical clinic, in which Carol was then treating an average of close to one thousand patients per month. Intertribal warfare being virtually a thing of the past, Kayagar, Auyu and Asmat could now mingle freely with Sawi and Atohwaem around our clinic door. Beyond the clinic a long path of piled-up clay led to a jungle-style primary school where teachers provided by the Indonesian government had enrolled over eighty Sawi

children in basic reading, writing and arithmetic courses.

To one side stood the dwellings of four Dani evangelists who, along with their families, had volunteered to work side-by-side with us among the Sawi, ministering to eighteen villages scattered across more than six-hundred square miles of nearly impassable swamps. Supported by their own Dani churches in the distant central highlands, and equipped with Sawi word lists, grammar, cultural insights, literacy primers and translated Scriptures, they had already succeeded in establishing groups of believers in a number of areas where government help was still almost nonexistent. Newly literate themselves, they were also teaching many Sawi to read and write.

Our days of aloneness were ended.

The Christian world view was already sinking its roots deep into the Sawi mind. Men who once abused and even tortured their wives as subhuman chattels and slaves now openly acknowledged their rights as cherishable companions and helpmeets. Monogamy was replacing polygamy as the ideal for marriage, though polygamists still retained their plural wives.

Women who once indulged in moodiness, screaming tirades and highly abusive speech now manifested a compelling newness and warmth of personality. Children were no longer being primed for war. Strangers and even former enemies could now accept invitations to feasts without fear of *tuwi asonai man*. *Gefam ason* and the *waness* bind were now only bad memories.

Even before the arrival of firm government control,

Christian Sawi headmen were beginning to carry out some measure of civil law, although there were still many unbelievers who preferred to solve their local problems with bows, spears, and daggers. And whenever government officers and police patrols penetrated the Sawi domain, they found a respectful welcome from tribespeople who had already been well briefed concerning the policies and programs of civil government.

———————————————

One of the beliefs which the Sawi had inherited from the distant past was the belief that it was unwise to attempt anything their ancestors had not previously sanctioned. Of course, we had already done considerable violence to this ancient hang-up by hiring them to build the airstrip, the ironwood bridge over the Tumdu and a four-mile-long canal connecting the Kronkel with the next river system to the north. "Digging rivers is a job for the spirits, not for men!" they had whispered when I first suggested this latter project. Nevertheless they completed the canal within a month without suffering any supernatural repercussions.

But the biggest, most mind-stretching challenge yet came when I suggested building the "Sawidome." By 1972, Yohwi had returned and constructed a new village along one side of our airstrip. Seremeet likewise had welcomed an invitation to build along the other side of the airstrip, so now we were a community of four villages with a total population of about eight hundred.

Our meeting house, which had already been en-larged twice, was again far too small even for regular gatherings and could not accommodate even one-fifth of the people who thronged two or three times a year to our Christian "love-feasts." On such occasions we had to meet out-of-doors at the mercy of fickle tropi-cal weather. Thus we were made keenly aware of the need for a structure which could accommodate not only the needs of our rapidly growing fellowship at Kamur, but also the swelling crowds which flocked in from surrounding villages on special days.

"It should seat at least a thousand people," I ex-plained to the Sawi church elders. "And must be circular with a cone-shaped roof. Any other design in a building so large will be too weak for monsoon storms, considering the kind of materials we have to work with."

I was not saying anything about our lack of heavy equipment or the inexperience of the workmen who would be involved—the Sawi Christians, nor of the foreman who would supervise the operation—myself.

For several days the elders weighed my suggestion carefully. The decision was entirely theirs to make, the structure would be their property, not mine. They would need to gather and prepare thousands of poles, tens of thousands of sago leaves for thatch, hundreds of yards of tying vines and other jungle materials for the project. The only contribution from the Tuans' world would be three kegs of steel spikes for the main supports, tools to work with, a few sheets of second-hand aluminum roofing for the uppermost peak of the roof and technical supervision.

Finally they returned to me. "Do you really think we can build it?" they asked.

"Men like you who have a tradition of building soaring treehouses can do it," I replied. "If you had no such heritage, I wouldn't even suggest it. This project is simply an extension of the tradition your ancestors started."

The next Lord's Day the Sawi church leaders urged every believing man, woman and child in the congregation to join in the massive project.

"If we think only of ourselves, we can of course make do with a smaller building," Amhwi, the chief elder, explained. "But we together with the Tuan believe we should raise up a building large enough for the believers of all the villages and their friends to gather together under one roof, to hear God's Word and to enjoy this new spirit of oneness which He has given us, a oneness our ancestors never dreamed of.

"It will be a house of peace in which former enemies can sit down together at the Lord's table, and a house of prayer for the tribes around us who are still without God's Word."

"For this you must expect no wages from the Tuan," added another elder. "The Tuan brought God's Word to us, but now we ourselves must accept responsibility for its further advance. If you agree to help, let it be because you love God and want others to receive His Word!"

The response was immediate. A swelling cry of "*Asyfem! Asyfem!* Let's build it! Let's build it!" rose on all sides.

After the Lord's Supper, all the believers joined hands around the plot of ground chosen for the structure. With a spirit of keen anticipation, they dedicated themselves to God for the task. Next day, men began hewing the twenty-four ironwood pillars which would support the weight of the entire roof. Each pillar was twenty-two feet long and weighed over 150 pounds. This important part of the task took several weeks.

Then the builders searched through the jungle for twenty-four *sereg* poles averaging about forty feet in length. These were to be the main rafters, each of which would be cantilevered from the top of an ironwood pillar, sloping up at a steep angle toward the peak of the roof. At this point a long-awaited interruption halted the work for a while.

We had just received word by radio that a new RBMU missionary couple, John and Esther Mills from Canada, would arrive within a few days to share our work among the Sawi. The Christians scattered to the jungle to gather food for a welcoming feast. When at last John and Esther arrived by MAF plane, nearly a thousand Sawi raised a tumultuous cheer, followed by a massive celebration. Then we started work at once on completion of a new dwelling for the Mills.

When this was finished, we turned our attention again to the new conference building. While the Sawi men and women continued stockpiling hundreds of cut poles, John Mills tackled the task of joining the rafters to the ironwood pillars and bracing them securely. When this was completed, we marked off a circular area of ground seventy-five feet in diameter, dug out twenty-four holes spaced evenly along its circumference and inserted the base of an ironwood pillar into each hole.

Lacking the services of a large crane, we had to find a way to erect each lofty pillar-rafter and hold it steady at the correct angle until clay could be packed around its base. We accomplished this by tying about twelve long vines halfway up the rafter, and then assigning one man to hold each vine taut while others pushed the rafter up with forked poles. Once a rafter had been raised halfway, the men holding the vines were able to pull it up to a fully vertical position.

The men on the vines were also able to keep the rafters from swaying. Whenever a rafter began to lean toward the west, for example, two or three men on the east side would tug on their vines until it came back into an upright position. Similarly, if it leaned north, workers on the south side would correct its lean.

Within two days, all twenty-four cantilevered rafters were soaring high above our heads, leaning inward toward a common center from the tops of the ironwood pillars. I was somewhat dismayed. I had expected the tips of the rafters to dip downward under their own weight, and had made allowance for their curve in planning a roof about forty feet high at the center—the same height as a Sawi tree-house. But they did not curve.

Through some peculiar characteristic of the *sereg* poles, each rafter stayed perfectly straight, as if its upper tip had no weight at all. This meant that the peak of the roof would end up considerably higher than forty feet. Just how much higher I couldn't be sure. The Sawi talent for working fearlessly at treetop heights was going to be a critical factor in completing the project.

Now the second phase of the operation began—tying the rafters together into a rigid cone spanning eighty-two feet of airspace, yet strong enough to withstand the force of monsoon gales sometimes gusting to fifty miles per hour. I recalled an episode from the life of John Paton, a nineteenth century missionary to the New Hebrides: "In a short time the (church) building was completed, and very proud were the Aniwans of their handiwork. The church was sixty-two feet by twenty-four, and the wall was twelve feet high—a good serviceable, suitable building, which all hoped would last for many years.

"But alas! before long a terrific hurricane swept the island, and the church was levelled to the ground."[1] How much greater then might the danger be to our "Sawidome," with a floor area four times greater than the Aniwan structure?

To strengthen the shell, I instructed the workers to interweave horizontal poles in and out among the upward sloping rafters, much as one would weave a giant basket. For safety's sake we placed the poles so close together that it would be unlikely for a worker ever to slip between them. As expected, the closer we got to the peak of the roof, the more rigid the cone became. The Sawi were soon amazed to find themselves working fifty and even sixty feet in the air on a structure that refused to quiver even under the weight of twenty men jumping up and down.

The original forty-foot-long rafters, of course, had to be lengthened several times to bring the roof to a peak, which proved to be sixty-two feet above the ground. By extending the roof on the outside of the ironwood pillars, we increased the diameter of the building to eighty-seven feet, with a floor area of nearly six thousand square feet.

Later we raised a twenty-two-foot-tall aluminum spire to the peak of the building and fixed it firmly in place, increasing the total height to eighty-four feet. The spire weighed about three hundred pounds. Inching it up the forty-five degree slope to its lofty perch took about a half hour of heaving by thirty strong men, encouraged by the cheering of hundreds of people on the ground below.

Next we covered the massive roof with thatch made of sago leaves. This took two weeks.

Then we piled up nearly one thousand cubic yards of clay, raising the soil floor under the dome well above the highest flood level. We also shaped it into a huge concave bowl. And the area we excavated on the south side of the church later became—in the rainy seasons—a reflecting pool mirroring the great structure.

To complete the project, benches were needed to seat over one thousand persons. We had no sawmill, so Sawi believers hewed the several hundred boards required by hand.

In June, 1972, the Sawi Christians dedicated their newly completed conference building to the glory of

God. Though its thatch occasionally needs repair, the building already has withstood about a dozen monsoon storms without a quiver. And the Sawi themselves are unaware that they have constructed what is possibly the world's largest circular building of unmilled poles.

The ancient hangups no longer inhibit Christian Sawi. Finding the world of their forebears too small, the Sawi are shedding the ancient ancestral cocoon. Now new hopes, soaring like the pinnacle of their Sawidome, stir them toward new horizons both spiritual and secular.

Yet at the very core of their new world stands something peculiarly related to their own unique past—the story of a Peace Child. It is the story of a Peace Child who, in a very special way, has become their Peace Child, a Peace Child who fulfills their past and guides their future. He is the Strengthener of the second pillar, which was really always meant to be the first pillar.

Stephen, Shannon and Paul snuggled close to Carol, listening intently as she read from an old, much-handled book. It was the story of the return of the prodigal son:

"And so the son returned to his father, and the father, seeing him afar off, ran to meet him, and fell on his neck and kissed him. And the son lifted up his voice and wept."

Carol stopped to ask a question. "Tell me, Shannon, why do you think the son wept?"

My second son's blue eyes grew very thoughtful as he pondered the question. Suddenly he looked up brightly and said: "Because he fell on his neck!"

Carol, Stephen and I dissolved in laughter while Shannon and Paul stared at us in wide-eyed bewilderment.

Outside I heard the soft echo of a bamboo horn. Amhwi was calling the Christians together for an evening class. Leaving Carol and the boys to finish their story, I walked out across our moonlit lawn and followed the streams of people who were heading for Amhwi's class. Sitting down near the back of the crowded classroom, I listened as Amhwi read a passage of Scripture by the light of a small storm lantern, and listened with amazement as he drew a striking analogy to illustrate it:

"Remember what Kaiyo used to do to those who threatened to break the peace he had established. He pointed them to the *tarop* child, and said, 'If that child had died, you would be free to do whatever you want to do. But he is not dead. He is still alive, and I am the advocate who is responsible for peace. You may not break the peace! My hand is strong!'

"So also if anyone tempts us to do evil, we should say to him, 'Look here! God has placed the Spirit of His Peace Child, Jesus, within me. If that Peace Child had died or gone away and left me, I might be free to do the evil you suggest. But He is not dead! Nor has He deserted me! He still lives within me to keep me in the way of goodness, and His hand is strong! I am not free to do the evil you advise!'"

The response from his listeners was enthusiastic.

"Those are good words!" or "Yes, let's all answer just like that!" or "We understand!"

Amhwi continued: "And why is it that we no longer exchange *tarop* children among our villages? It is because God would be offended. He would say, 'Isn't My Peace Child good enough? Do you think you have to add your own children to Him?' "

Quietly I slipped out again into the cool night and headed home. Soon I passed the little office where I had labored countless hours on the intricacies of the Sawi language and was now laboring again to complete the translation of the Sawi New Testament. Memories began to flood back, memories that drew me aside into a narrow path branching toward the Tumdu.

I followed the path until it ended on the crest of a knoll of high ground beside the still river. I stared down at the dew-wet *kunai* grass around me, remembering the two men who lay buried beneath it. Two men whom I had learned to love very deeply. Two men who in their lifetime had often looked into me with a closeness of understanding rare on earth.

One was Kaiyo. He had been killed four years earlier, an unexpected victim of a sudden flareup of violence within Kamur village itself. But the lessons he taught me lived on.

The other? I recalled the day three years earlier when Carol and I had returned from a journey to learn that Hato had died of pneumonia during our absence. So quickly, he was gone.

The one-eyed stranger first to touch my hand in that leafy arena which had since become my home;

the friend who trusted me even when he couldn't understand; the seeker who so quickly grasped the Mystery that was seeking him.

Aeons of change had metamorphosed us both until we appeared totally alien to each other. Yet providence had brought us together again. Why? To demonstrate that Christ is the Fulfiller of *every* man's true self.

I turned slowly from the two unmarked graves and walked along the grassy edge of the Tumdu. Peace seemed to be everywhere and in everything. It was flowing down with the moonlight, twinkling through the stars, shimmering among reflections. It vibrated through birdcalls and Amhwi's now distant voice.

It brought back the memory of another voice which, though now hushed in death, still echoed out of that very different world from which we had come; the firm, commissioning voice of an old, white-haired man:

"You will encounter customs and beliefs which will baffle you, but which must be understood. . . .

"Our Lord is impatient to establish His kingdom of love in those dark places which are now the habitation of cruelty. . . .

"Who will go?"

I reached for the gate, and as I touched it, joy swept through me. Joy more than just my own.

FOOTNOTES

1. Charles D. Michael, *John Gibson Paton, D.D.* (Kilmarnock, Scotland: John Ritchie Ltd.), p. 134.

Author's Postscript

The six Asmat men lie face down, side by side on a grass mat in the center of a manhouse. Three of them are regular occupants of that manhouse. The others are former enemies from a distant village who have come to make peace. The six wives of the six men stand spread-legged among their prone husbands, each wife with one foot tucked under her own husband's chest and the other under his hip, while her heels touch the chest and hip of the man lying behind her.

Now the elders of both villages bring six wide-eyed children, three from each of the two negotiating communities, into the manhouse. The children are beautifully decorated in woven armbands and tassels of shredded sago frond fibers. One by one they are

instructed to get down on their faces and stomachs and squirm through over the backs of the six fathers below and between the ankles of the six mothers above. As each child emerges through that canal of human flesh, he or she is picked up and rocked and lullabied like a newborn baby.

The passage formed by the bodies of the six fathers and mothers is a symbolic *communal* birth canal, through which the three children from each side have been reborn into the kinship system of the enemy village. As long as they live, they will form a vital bond between the two villages, keeping them from war.

Peace through a new birth experience!

A missionary working among the Western Danis of Irian Jaya (Indonesia's new name for the former Netherlands New Guinea or West Irian) has just discovered how to put two very important words together. One is *ki,* "life." The other is *wone,* "words."

Outside his office door, a vast assembly of fierce-looking Dani men are seated, pigtusk and cowrie shell ornaments gleaming brightly on their black skin and smoke-darkened hair nets.

Uncertainly, the missionary emerges from his office to try out his new phrase. Raising his hands above his head he calls for silence and then shouts in halting Dani: "We have come to bring you *ki wone,* the words of life!"

He did not know that with just one sentence he could touch off a revolution. Its beginning was almost imperceptible, for the younger men and children were paying little attention to the strange sayings of this alien from beyond the farthest mountains.

But some of the older Dani men caught the phrase. Grizzled old sages turned and stared at the white man, blinking as if waking from an agelong sleep. Deep within their beings a spring that had been coiled aeons ago began to unwind, triggering a subtle, wonder-producing mechanism. Their mouths gaped, already beginning to shape the pronouncement that had been delayed so long. Trembling with excitement as they leaned upon their staffs, the sages conferred with one another.

"His skin is white just like the new skin of a snake after it has shed its old skin," said one man.

"And he's talking about *ki wone!*" exclaimed a second.

"It is happening just as our ancestors said it would!" wheezed a third. "When immortality returns to mankind, those who learn its secret first will come over the mountains and tell you that secret. Their skins will be white, because they are constantly being renewed like the skin of a snake. Be sure you listen to them when they come, otherwise *nabelan-kabelan*—'my-skin-your-skin,' or 'immortality'—will pass by you!' "

The missionary was now busy at other tasks, still not aware of the awakening that was gathering momentum around him. That night, when the whole valley burst forth into singing, he began to wonder what sort of celebration was taking place.

Next morning thousands of Danis surrounded his

home, asking, "How should we welcome the words of life?"

Redemptive analogies, God's keys to man's cultures, are the New Testament-approved approach to cross-cultural evangelism. And only in the New Testament do we find the pattern for discerning and appropriating them, a pattern we must learn to use.

Some redemptive analogies stand out in the legends and records of the past: Olenos the Sinbearer; Balder the Innocent, hounded to his death, yet destined to rule the new world; Socrates' *Righteous Man;* the god of the Athenians, an analogy appropriated by the apostle Paul; The Logos, appropriated by the apostle John; the sacrificial lamb of the Hebrews, appropriated by both John the Baptist and Paul.

Other redemptive analogies have been found hidden away in the cultures of the present—dormant, residual, waiting: the Sawi *tarop* child and the words of *remon*; *nabelan-kabelan,* the Dani tribe's deep-seated hope of immortality; the Asmat new birth ceremony. Still others are the places of refuge and the legends of the fall of man, of the Deluge, and of a "ladder" connecting earth and heaven.

How many more are yet waiting to be found, waiting to be appropriated for the deliverance of the people who believe them, waiting to be supplanted by Christ, that they may then fade from sight behind the brilliance of His glory, having fulfilled their God-ordained purpose?

Only those who go and search will find them.